**KEY TEXT
REFERENCE**

SHARING
NATURE with
CHILDREN II

A Sequel to the Classic Parents' & Teachers'
Nature Awareness Guidebook

SHARING NATURE with CHILDREN II

JOSEPH CORNELL

Formerly SHARING THE JOY OF NATURE

DAWN PUBLICATIONS

P.O. Box 2010 • Nevada City • California 95959 • USA

To those
who share the joy
of nature

Copyright © 1989 by Joseph Cornell

Library of Congress Cataloguing-in-Publication Data
Cornell, Joseph Bharat
   Sharing nature with children II / by Joseph Cornell.
p. cm
ISBN: 1-883220-87-4
1. Nature study. 2. Nature study—Activity programs. 3. Natural history—Study and teaching.. 4. Natural history—study and teaching—Activity programs. I Title.
QH51.C78 1989   508—dc20

DAWN PUBLICATIONS
P.O. Box 2010
Nevada City, CA 95959
800-545-7475
email: nature@dawnpub.com
website: www.dawnpub.com

16 15 14 13 12 11 10 9 8
First Edition
Printed in the United States of America
on recycled paper.

CONTENTS

FOREWORD

I HAVE BEEN READING and rereading Joseph Cornell's books for ten years. They worked marvelously for me in my role as a school teacher and principal. They've also served as a continuing source of lasting personal inspiration.

Over the years, I've discovered that children learn far more effectively if the teacher can imbue the learning experience with a sense of joy. The wonderful methods described in Joseph Cornell's books help teachers do just that. I'm convinced that teachers, youth leaders, naturalists, and parents will find in them new ways to introduce children and adults to the joy of learning.

A telling insight into the mission of this gentle man: Some years ago, Joseph was working as a nature-education consultant in the Grand Canyon, when he decided to spend a few quiet hours one morning absorbing the spectacular view from the South Rim. He chose a popular spot, one that attracted a continuing flow of tourists. To his amazement, Joseph saw that few of the tourists were spending more than a few seconds actually looking at the Canyon, before turning to fiddle with cameras, talk with friends, and head back to their cars. Of approximately 150 people who visited the overlook, he saw only three who appeared to be gazing intently for longer than thirty seconds at one of Earth's most magnificent natural scenes.

Although Joseph felt most of the tourists were quite sincere in their appreciation, they lacked the special skills a person needs to fully absorb nature's beauty and magnificence. This compassionate observation is typical of Joseph, for he deeply believes that anyone can develop the ability to draw inspiration from nature, whether in the form of the Grand Canyon or a humble oak tree in one's own back yard.

Joseph's joyous enthusiasm for nature is contagious. I recently watched while he led a presentation at an environmental fair on the West Coast. He is a humble spirit who makes few demands concerning his presentations. His presence was not particularly highlighted; the program guide gave the usual information regarding topic, time, and location. Like the many other presenters, Joseph was assigned to a small classroom. Numerous presentations were being given simultaneously.

I remember most vividly what happened when nearly three hundred people showed up at the classroom, which was big enough for just forty people. Joseph smiled and said there was enough room for everyone. His concern was clearly that some people might get discouraged and leave. As the crowd grew, it became apparent that nearly everyone at the fair wanted to hear Joseph speak. He beckoned to the audience to follow and led us outside to an open space and began sharing his nature activities, teaching philosophy and methods for "listening to nature." At the end of the talk, the feeling in the group was so wonderful that none of us wanted to leave. We all knew we'd found a friend who could show us how to experience more deeply the harmony and beauty of life.

Readers familiar with Joseph's two other books, *Sharing Nature with Children* and *Listening to Nature*, will be pleased to find much deeper insights into his methods in this book. The stages of Joseph's teaching philosophy, **Flow Learning**, which are alluded to in *Sharing Nature with Children*, are developed here in much greater depth.

I have implemented the concepts of Flow Learning in my own teaching with wonderful results. Flow Learning embraces tested educational principles, and is by no means limited to outdoor education. The Flow Learning principles can be used in academic and artistic fields, as well. They can also be used in virtually any setting to build group cohesiveness.

This new volume is user-friendly and goof-proof. The carefully designed stages of Flow Learning make it easy for parents and teachers to choose activities appropriate to any group's age, mood, and physical environment. The games create an almost magical atmosphere of wholesome fun. Universal in its appeal and usefulness, *Sharing Nature with Children II* is indeed a worthy sequel to *Sharing Nature with Children*.

—DR. JAY CASBON, *Educator*

PREFACE

S HARING NATURE WITH CHILDREN, a guide to forty-two nature-awareness activities, was published in 1979. [*Editor's note:* a second edition to *Sharing Nature with Children,* expanded to 50 activities, was published in 1998.] This second volume, a sequel and companion to the earlier one, offers activities developed during the intervening years. All of them rank high on my list of favorites. But more importantly, *Sharing Nature with Children II* provides a fuller development of the **Flow Learning** system of nature awareness. Flow Learning helps teachers, parents, or nature guides tune into a group's level of enthusiasm (or boredom!) and sensitively leads them into energized, enjoyable appreciation of the natural world. I think you'll find it a practical, commonsense, easy-to-use tool.

You won't have to read the first volume of *Sharing Nature with Children* before using this book. I did find it necessary to refer to games described in *Sharing Nature with Children,* but whenever this occurred I provided a short description of the game. If you think you might like to play the game, though, you will find it very helpful to look up the full description in *Sharing Nature with Children.*

Another book, *Listening to Nature,* offers reflective, inspirational nature activities intended primarily for adults, although many of the activities could also be used with adolescents in connection with stage three of the Flow Learning system. Though published before *Sharing Nature with Children II,* it was intended to be read after this book.

Chapter I

LEARNING WITH
THE HEART

O N A BRILLIANT DAY of blue sky and white, puffy clouds, I led a group of children out into the woods. A storm had just broken, and light streaming between the clouds illuminated the forest, making everything glow with life. Even the animals seemed to be exulting in the fresh vitality that follows a storm, because we saw them everywhere.

The group seemed a bit large, with 37 children, for a sensitive and profound nature experience. But the magic of the towering, sunlit trees and brightly flowered meadows worked its spell. The children spread out spontaneously and moved through the forest in small groups. Each party of explorers made discovery after discovery, until I could barely keep up with the children's urgent calls, questions, and exclamations of delight.

That afternoon stands in my memory as a particularly satisfying experience of sharing nature deeply with others. When we, as leaders, can provide an atmosphere of sensitive discovery and direct experience, nature is able to change people's lives spontaneously, in wonderful ways.

On that particular hike, I saw just such a change occur in Jack, one of the younger boys. At home, Jack was a hunter. He frequently shot songbirds, thinking of them merely as challenging moving targets. The fact that the birds were living beings simply wasn't a reality to Jack, and, of course, he didn't know about the laws against shooting songbirds.

At the end of our hike I asked the children to lie on their backs and gaze up at the spreading branches of a large oak tree. While we were enjoying the tree from this unique perspective, we heard the "tsit-tsit" call of a flock of bushtits—tiny, grayish-brown, long-tailed songbirds—in the nearby trees. I taught the children a simple but effective bird call, which we promptly began to use. (See "Bird Calling" in *Sharing Nature with Children*.)

Bushtits and other small songbirds readily respond to this call, and we weren't disappointed. The flock of about twenty-five bushtits flitted closer and closer through the branches until they were just a few feet above us. The bushtits' and children's calls attracted other nearby birds. Soon, Western tanagers, mountain chickadees, nuthatches, and warblers were hopping about in the oak tree above us. The children were astonished by the colorful spectacle of so many birds singing and flitting from branch to branch nearby.

Over fifty birds responded to our calls, and the excited children wanted to know the names of all of them. When a robin-sized, red-faced, yellow and black bird appeared, I told them, "That's a western tanager! He's flown all the way from Mexico or Central America to raise his family here in these woods." Most of the other birds, too, stayed long enough for me to share interesting facts about them.

While we watched from close up, each bird became individually alive for the children. For the rest of the week there was high interest in birds. Even Jack was deeply touched by the experience, and whenever we spotted a new bird, he was among the first with questions about its name and habits. His attitude toward birds had completely changed. Jack began to treasure them as fascinating fellow forms of life.

The distinguished botanist, Liberty Hyde Bailey, who founded the nature-study movement at the turn of the century, said, "Sensitiveness to life is the highest product of education." If we want to develop an attitude of reverence for life, we need to begin with awareness, which in turn can lead to loving empathy. As we begin to feel our common bond of life with living things around us, our actions become more harmonious in an unforced, natural way, and we become concerned for the needs and well-being of all creatures. As the eminent Japanese conservationist Tanaka Shozo put it, "The care of rivers is not a question of rivers, but of the human heart."

But simple exposure to nature isn't always enough. A friend of mine discovered this when he took his eight-year-old son hiking in the Canadian Rockies. They hiked for several hours until they came to a spectacular overlook, from where they could see out over two glaciated valleys and several alpine lakes.

He recalls, "That view alone made the long trip worthwhile!" He wanted his son to share his joy in the mountain scenery, so he suggested they sit and enjoy the view. But the boy, who'd been running exuberantly back and forth along the trail while they hiked, sat for five seconds, then scrambled to his feet and started running up the trail again. My friend said he felt like screaming. Knowing what his son was missing, he was frustrated by his inability to communicate the experience.

We who love natural surroundings enjoy sharing our delight and would like to know how best to transmit our inspirations to others. But, like my friend, we sometimes find it isn't easy—I know I, too, faced difficult challenges when I was just starting out as an outdoor educator. Most challenging of all was the problem of focusing children's lively energies so that I could lead them into nature experiences that were deep, subtle, and filled with joyous inner meanings.

Through years of trial and error, I developed a set of insights into teaching that now play a central role in my work. You may already be using these principles, yourself. Perhaps you, too, stumbled across them intuitively, as I did, and perhaps you know them by another name. In any case, they can make your nature classes more dynamic, fun, and deeply inspiring. Since becoming aware of these principles, I've been able to accomplish my highest goals as a nature educator, with amazing consistency.

In clarifying the principles for myself and others, I found that they fit together in a wonderfully systematic, flexible way. I call this collection of methods *Flow Learning*, because it describes a way to use nature-awareness activities in a flowingly purposeful, directional way. The beauty of Flow Learning is that it shows you how to begin *where your students are*, then rouse their enthusiastic participation and guide them, step by step, through increasingly sensitive activities and deep experiences into new, joy-filled awareness and understanding. Because it's extremely simple and effective, I believe you'll find Flow Learning a delight to use.

Chapter II

FLOW LEARNING
NATURAL STEPS TO NATURE
AWARENESS

I N LEADING NATURE ACTIVITIES over the years, I gradually realized that there was a sequence for using games and activities that always seemed to work best, regardless of a group's age, its mood, or the physical setting. I became convinced that the reason people responded so well to this particular sequence was that it's in harmony with certain subtle aspects of human nature.

In time, I blended all the outdoor activities I'd ever collected or created into this natural way of teaching. I've been using it now for almost ten years with great success, in tremendously varied situations, and with groups of many nationalities, ages, and backgrounds.

I call the system Flow Learning, because it has four stages that flow from one into another in a smooth, natural way:

STAGE 1: Awaken **Enthusiasm**
STAGE 2: Focus **Attention**
STAGE 3: Direct **Experience**
STAGE 4: Share **Inspiration**

Let's look at the stages one by one:

STAGE 1: Without **enthusiasm**, you can never have a meaningful experience of nature. By enthusiasm, I'm not talking about wild-eyed, jumping-up-and-down excitement, but a calm, intense flow of personal interest and keen alertness. Without this kind of enthusiasm, we learn very little.

STAGE 2: Learning depends on focused **attention**. Enthusiasm alone isn't enough. If our thoughts are scattered, we can't be dynamically aware—of nature, or anything else. So we must bring our enthusiasm to a calm focus.

STAGE 3: As we gradually focus our attention, we become more aware of what we're seeing, hearing, touching, smelling, and receiving through intuition. With calm attention, we can enter more sensitively into the rhythm and flow of nature all around us.

Focused attention creates an inner calmness and openness that allows us to experience nature directly, without the interference of static from the mind. So the third stage is absorbing **direct experience**.

STAGE 4: Experience opens up deeper awareness. What do I mean by this? In *Sharing Nature with Children* I described a game called Still Hunting, where the player remains very, very still while nature returns to its normal routine all around. Let's imagine that you're still hunting and birds land very close in a tree overhead. By remaining still, you begin to feel a kind of breathless oneness with life all around you, almost as if you were blending into the scene and experiencing life through the birds, the grass, and the waving branches of the trees. In that stillness, you can sometimes feel a great, bursting joy or a deep, calm happiness, or an overwhelming sense of the beauty or power of creation. Nature *is* always inspiring, and it's only our restless minds that keep us from being more often joyfully aware of this.

A leader can help a group deepen its inspiration by telling stories about nature that uplift and inspire, or by telling stories from the lives of the great naturalists and conservationists, such as Rachel Carson, John Muir, Aldo Leopold, and Henry David Thoreau.

I call the fourth stage sharing **inspiration**, because sharing strengthens and clarifies our own deep experiences.

LEARNING WITH A NATURAL FLOW

Flow Learning allows you to create an endless variety of nature experiences, each ideally matched to present circumstances and no two ever exactly alike. Although it's based on a few simple principles, it's not a rigid system of activities that you always have to do the same way. You can use Flow Learning with the games and activities from my books, and with any other resources you may know.

I've used Flow Learning successfully in sessions that lasted from 30 minutes to all day. I've used it indoors in rainy weather and outdoors in the sun. It's very flexible, because it gives you the freedom to respond appropriately to the needs of the moment. The goal of Flow Learning is to give everyone a genuinely uplifting experience of nature. After a successful Flow Learning session, each person feels a subtle, enjoyable new awareness of his oneness with nature and an increased empathy with all of life. You'll find, too, that people will listen much more enthusiastically to discussions of the scientific side of natural history and ecology if you first help them get into a receptive and inspired mood.

A Successful Flow Hike

Several years ago, a local school asked me to lead a nature-awareness hike for a small elementary-age class. On the scheduled day, the weather was miserably hot. As if that weren't enough of a challenge, my session was scheduled for just after lunch; it was the last day of the school year; and the children, who'd been up very late the night before, were listless and cranky. When the teacher announced that it was time to go outdoors and play nature games, they could barely muster the energy to groan, "I don't want to." "It's too hot outside." "I'm tired." "Do we *have* to?!"

I had invited a photographer to come along and take pictures, and I was beginning to feel less than optimistic about the results. The accompanying photo leaves no doubt about the children's initial apathy.

A hot, June day, with tired and unwilling children—an inauspicious beginning!

Look at the change in body postures and facial expressions—the Animal Parts Game has awakened their enthusiasm. Here they're acting out a scorpion.

I realized that before anything else could happen, I'd have to help the children rise out of their sleepy indifference. I bustled them outdoors, and we started playing a game called Animal Parts. The children chose an animal, and I asked them each to take the role of one of the animal's parts. They chose a scorpion, and as they joined together to form the body, moving around and acting out the scorpion's typical behavior, their energy and enthusiasm began to rise. (Complete instructions for Animal Parts are given in *Sharing Nature with Children*.) They were no longer complaining or standing on one leg in heavy, silent protest. Soon they were having so much fun that they were eagerly looking forward to the other games.

We then played Pyramid of Life, a Stage 1 (Enthusiasm) game that demonstrates food chains. At the lowest level of the food chain are the plants, next are herbivores (plant-eaters), then predators (meat-eaters).

We're solidly on our way. The children are thoroughly enjoying Pyramid of Life, through which they're learning about food chains.

In Pyramid of Life, you ask the children to name a plant, herbivore, or predator that they want to play. The trick is not to tell them that you're going to ask them to build a human pyramid with plants on the bottom and lions and tigers at the top! (Complete instructions are given in *Sharing Nature With Children*. Be careful to build the pyramid on soft ground, to cushion the inevitable collapse at the end of the game. And don't build a pyramid more than three levels high. Children with physical problems can help steady the pyramid and help the others get into position.)

Because it was too hot for yet another vigorous game, and because the children were enjoying themselves and seemed ready for more sensitive and reflective experiences, we next played a Stage 2 (Attention) activity: the Sounds Game. In this game, the children close their eyes for one or two minutes and raise a finger every time they hear a sound coming from nature. They then discuss the sounds they've heard. (For details, see *Sharing Nature With Children*.)

In the Sounds Game we focus our attention on the natural sounds around us.

The Camera Game is always a favorite, giving fresh experiences of nature.

We then played the Camera Game, a Stage 3 (Experience) activity. The group divided up in pairs, one child playing photographer and the other playing camera. The "camera" kept its eyes closed until the photographer "took a picture" of some beautiful or interesting natural object or scene by pressing on the camera's ear for three to five seconds while the camera opened its "shutter" (eyes). The cameras saw the world in a fresh and interesting way, because the time of observation was too short for distracting thoughts to intrude. (For further details, see page 104.)

The Mystery Animal Game has aroused the children's active interest in a new animal. Here they're involved in studying its picture.

As the accompanying photos reveal, the children were involved by now and were having a great time. The temperature was well over a hundred degrees, so we retired to a cool grove of oak and madrone trees. We now chose a quiet Stage 3 activity (Experience) called Mystery Animal. (See page 85.) In Mystery Animal, you ask the group to close their eyes while you describe an animal, without revealing its name. (You should choose an animal that has an interesting physical appearance and behavior.) In your narrative, you take your listeners on an imaginary trip to the land where the animal lives, showing them its natural habitat and telling them what the animal looks like, how it gets food, how it spends its time, and so on. When you finish your story, you pass out paper and pencils, and the players try to draw the animal from your verbal description.

Mystery Animal captures attention powerfully in groups of children or adults. The element of mystery makes the players extremely curious about the animal, and they listen with keen attention while trying to discover the animal's identity. In the process, they learn a great deal.

The children in our group sat completely still while I described the animal. When I took out a picture of a desert kangaroo rat, they came forward and studied it with intense interest to see how closely it resembled their drawings.

By now the children were feeling relaxed and receptive, so I ended the class with exciting and inspiring episodes from the life of John Muir.

We ended the day with inspiring stories from the lives of great naturalists.

How Flow Learning Can Work for You

Outdoors, there are any number of distractions that can prevent your group from becoming aware of its surroundings. Aside from distractions like cars, machinery, and even human voices, they may be feeling cold, or they may be worried about personal problems. A great strength of Flow Learning is that it helps people free their attention so they can relax, have fun, and enjoy the natural world.

The strong central current of a river carries away the sluggish eddies that form along the river's banks. Similarly, when you introduce people to nature with playful activities that energize body and mind, the high energy that the games develop washes away personal problems and moods. Freed from personal worries, their enthusiasm and attention can flow into new and fascinating experiences.

FOUR STEPS
TO NATURE AWARENESS

*Let's take a closer look
at Flow Learning,
and see
which kinds of activities work
best for each stage.*

STAGE 1:
AWAKEN ENTHUSIASM

"Nothing is so contagious as enthusiasm. . . . it is the genius of sincerity, and truth accomplishes no victories without it."
—BULWER-LYTTON

As the name suggests, this stage is playful. Fun-filled games and activities create a lively flow of energy. You'll know you've met the goal of this stage when you realize that everyone is playing with joyful enthusiasm.

In *Sharing Nature with Children*, I called the activities of Stage 1 "Otter" games, because the otter is the only animal that plays throughout its adult life. Through shared fun, the Enthusiasm stage gives people a feeling of closeness with one another. It creates a base of alertness and enthusiasm on which you can build subtler, more meaningful learning experiences.

When you lead nature outings, it's extremely important to get off to a good start, because people generally decide within a few minutes whether they're going to have a good time. By starting with lively games, you're far more likely to get the group's whole-hearted participation.

Many people resist anything new. To get them to participate enthusiastically in sensitive nature activities, you'll first have to convince them that they're going to have a good time—in other words, that in this case at least, "new" is going to equal "fun." The first stage accomplishes this. Grownups and teenagers are more likely than young children to adopt a cool, wait-and-see stance, but I've seen the power of the Stage 1 games win over even very skeptical groups.

Wild Animal Scramble and the Animal Clue Game are excellent for breaking the ice and encouraging passive groups to participate fully. Wild Animal Scramble is wonderful for creating an atmosphere of fun. To play, you pin a picture of an animal on each person's back, then you tell them to ask the other players questions until they find out which animal they are. Few people can remain coolly detached while everyone else is laughing and hooting at the skunk or buzzard pinned to their back. (For complete instructions, see *Sharing Nature with Children*.) The Animal Clue Game, described later in this book, works well too, and takes less time than Wild Animal Scramble.

Elementary-age children nearly always have plenty of energy. The Enthusiasm stage provides a structure for their high energy. After you've gotten their attention with several spirited Stage 1 games, you can refine the level of fun with subtler activities. Once they realize you're a person who knows how to have fun, they'll listen eagerly to your suggestions.

The attention-focusing effect of these playful games deflects potential discipline problems before they occur. The children become so engrossed in having fun that they have no time for mischief.

The magical power of the first-stage games never ceases to amaze me. I experienced this with a group in Japan, where the games worked their spell in spite of the awkwardness of having to speak through a translator. The group, all adults, stood listening politely to the translator with solemn faces. After a short introductory talk, I explained Wild Animal Scramble. Not knowing what to expect from this gravely courteous group, I was relieved and delighted when at one point during the translation every somber face broke into a smile of joyful expectation. I could almost feel the energy of the group shoot up, establishing a tone of lively enthusiasm that lasted throughout the day.

Later, the adults watched while I worked with a group of fifteen sweet-natured second-grade girls and five ten-year-old boys. The boys were a little wild—pushing and boxing each other and making a steady patter of smart remarks.

To establish a mood of fun and cooperation, I first had to capture the boys' interest. I cut short their banter by briskly hustling the children into a circle. With the circle formed and the children holding hands, I had at least the outward appearance of control. I introduced the game of Bat and Moth, choosing the five boys to play Moths while I played Bat. As I "flew" around the inside of the circle blindfolded, I had only my "sonar" to guide me to my prey, the Moths. Every time I called out "Bat!", they had to cry "Moth!" while I tried to tag them. This created lots of excitement among the Moths, and it was tremendously entertaining for the girls. The game took about 10 minutes, and by the end all the children were having a great time. They were eager to find out what I had to offer next. (For full details of Bat and Moth, see *Sharing Nature with Children*.)

These experiences show how important it is to choose your first activities carefully, with sensitive awareness of the group's special needs. Wild Animal Scramble gave the adults an amusing, energy-raising challenge without bending their dignity. The adults might not have related as well to the rowdy, child-oriented energy of Bat and Moth. But if I had tried Wild Animal Scramble with the children, the boys would have had far too much time to get into mischief.

As you become familiar with the games and gain experience with groups of varied ages, you'll find it increasingly easy to sense a group's needs and choose appropriate activities.

STAGE 2
FOCUS ATTENTION

As a young boy, George Washington Carver, the great botanist, was a keen observer of nature. In fact, he became known in his home town as "the plant doctor" for his remarkable ability to know exactly what was wrong with a plant and, by sensitively understanding its needs, to prescribe a cure. People were amazed by Carver's knowledge, particularly since, as a freed slave, he had never had any schooling.

To little George Carver, it was all very simple. When people expressed amazement at his skill, he would say, "They just *look* at their flowers. They don't *see* them, else they'd know what's wrong good as me."

If we give complete attention to what we're observing, like George Washington Carver we can see nature in fresh, new ways. At the close of the Enthusiasm stage, people are usually having lots of fun and feeling relaxed and enthusiastic. Now you can begin to bring that energy to a fine focus, with games that help people become calmly, enthusiastically attentive. The games of Stage 2 (Attention) help develop calmness and receptivity.

To free our attention for nature, we need to quiet our minds. But if you introduce quiet, sensitive activities too soon, many people will still be too restless to enjoy them. The Attention stage serves as a bridge between energetic, playful games and games that call for quiet, focused attention.

The games of the Attention stage are simple but remarkably effective. Not only do they help people become more observant, they also help attune heart and mind to nature's beauty.

You'll find it easy to make up your own Attention games that are

every bit as effective as the ones I describe in this book. The key is to isolate one of the senses (touch, sight, hearing) and devise a clever way to help the players concentrate on it.

A good example of a game that uses the sense of sight is Unnature Trail. In this game, you place man-made objects along a trail, and the players try to see how many they can find. Some objects are easy to see, while others (a large, rusty nail) are harder because they blend with the natural surroundings.

You should place the objects so that the players need to be intently aware to discover them all, thus developing observational skills while focusing their attention. A teacher told me she once forgot to mark the end of an Unnature Trail that was about 80 feet long, and that her students kept looking with keen interest for another 200 yards before she realized what had happened and tracked them down! (Unnature Trail is described in detail in *Sharing Nature with Children*.)

One of my favorite Attention activities is the Sounds Game. To play, you tell the group to find a comfortable spot and sit down, not too far apart, then close their eyes and hold up their fists. Every time they hear a sound, they raise a finger. Let them listen for about two minutes, then have them take turns describing the sounds they've heard. The Sounds Game is short and sweet, but very effective for concentrating the players' minds. It also helps them settle down after the playful first stage, in preparation for storytelling or a talk on natural history. And it gives people a fresh awareness of nature's interesting and beautiful sounds.

Another favorite of mine is the Sound Map, described in detail later in the book. You give the players a 4 × 6 card and pencil, then ask them to sit far enough apart that they feel alone. On the card, the player draws a map with an X in the center, indicating where he's sitting. When he hears a sound, he marks it on the map, carefully judging the sound's direction and distance. The marks should not be literal drawings, but should look like a "picture" of the sound. What's important is not so much how the sounds are drawn as the players' deep attention and focus on listening. Like the Sounds Game, the Sound Map simply and naturally helps the players become more sensitively aware of the immediate environment.

The Attention stage needn't last long—5–15 minutes is plenty. (Feel free to set time limits for the games that seem appropriate for the natural setting and age and mood of the players.) If the surroundings are really spectacular—thousands of waterfowl flying overhead at a waterfowl refuge, for example—you might not have to use any Stage 2 (Attention) games at all. The magic of the environment will seize the group's attention, and your challenge will be the enjoyable one of helping them absorb the setting as fully as possible.

What do you do if you find yourself, as I sometimes have, faced with the challenge of giving 30 children a meaningful experience of nature in a concrete inner-city playground that has a single, scrawny tree? You may need to devote a lot of time to waking up their interest, before you can begin helping them to see the tree in new ways. (By the way, if you ever do find yourself in such a situation, you might try some of the tree activities described later in the book.)

The important thing in Stage 2 is to be intensely aware of the group's level of enthusiasm and receptivity. Ask yourself, "Are they ready for more sensitive experiences yet?" If not, then ask, "What games can I use to raise their enthusiasm and focus their attention?"

STAGE 3
DIRECT EXPERIENCE

*"No amount of word-making will ever make
a single soul know these mountains . . . See how
willingly Nature poses herself upon photographers' plates. [Yet]
no earthy chemicals are so sensitive as those of the human soul.
All that is required is exposure, and purity of material."*

—JOHN MUIR

In a forest at dusk, fifteen teenagers and I were walking barefoot along a trail in almost total silence, feeling the tranquility of the coming night. Because we were quiet and unobtrusive, the animals we saw seemed unafraid. After brief, curious looks, they calmly went about their affairs. Because of the serenity of the evening and the poise and naturalness of the animals, we felt a special sense of harmony and a kinship with the world.

While we walked I noticed that a boy named Gary was intently watching the bats that swooped and fluttered around us. Later, when we talked about our experiences, Gary said he'd been very frightened by bats, but that in the peace of the night he discovered he could watch them without fear. He said that, in fact, he'd been enjoying the grace and beauty of their flight.

Gary's calm openness that evening enabled him to transcend his fear of bats and begin to appreciate them. Many times in my own life, and in working with others, I've seen how a direct experience can open a person's heart. That's why, when I take a group to an area, I look over the terrain and choose settings that lend themselves to powerful, direct experiences. I then steer all the activities toward giving the group an experience of a particular aspect of the surroundings. To give an example:

Some thirty friends and I went on a picnic in the California Redwoods. I felt that everyone wanted to "connect" in some way with these magnificent trees. I set up a rope trail and led them blindfolded to many interesting places which they explored with hands, ears, and noses. I planned the rope trail playfully; it was full of adventurous twists and turns. The players squeezed through clumps of closely-growing redwoods, walked by a cascading stream, and passed in and out of brightly-lit forest clearings.

Finally, they came to the highlight of the trail. It was dark and very, very quiet. Some thought they'd entered a cave. No longer could they hear birds singing, or the wind. The ground felt hard under their feet. As they walked forward, they had to crouch, then crawl, over a hard, polished surface. On and on they followed the rope into the unknown. Some became anxious, but I reassured them that they were safe and encouraged them to go on. They proceeded cautiously, with outstretched arms. As the opening became smaller and smaller, they felt rough walls. Several times the silence was broken by exclamations of gleeful recognition as some person in the group realized where we were. Finally, the rope led out through a small, square opening into dazzling sunlight.

We returned to the start of the trail, where they took off their blindfolds and followed the rope again to see where they had been. Those who hadn't already guessed were delighted to find that they had passed through a huge, hollow, fallen redwood. They had entered at the base and walked and crawled nearly forty feet to emerge through a window cut in the tree's side. They were stunned by the tree's immense size, and spent a long time examining it closely.

If I had simply led them to the tree and talked about its age, weight, and reproductive habits, they might have expressed mild interest; they might even have felt it with their hands and thought about it a bit in an abstract sort of way. But having experienced it as a mystery, they were astounded by this gigantic, ancient, once-living thing that had not too long ago crashed to the forest floor. Many of my friends spent a long time just sitting quietly with this primeval, fallen giant.

Although Stage 3 (Direct Experience) and Stage 2 (Focus Attention) are similar, they differ in the greater power of the Direct

Experience games to involve people directly in nature. For example, shutting off people's sense of sight makes them much more alert to information from the other senses, and so helps them experience their surroundings in fresh ways. Each of the Direct Experience activities is designed to intensify one or more sense-elements of the nature experience. See, for example, the Bird Calling and Blind Trail activities in *Sharing Nature with Children*, and the Camera Game in this book.

You can give people deeply inspiring experiences of nature even in

public parks. All it takes is a little creativity. The Flow Learning technique was developed with difficult situations like these in mind. If it's raining and you have to come indoors, you can still use all the stages of Flow Learning. There are many activities that give the players enjoyable "nature-experiences" with the help of the imagination. For examples, see Tree Imagery and Mystery Animal, later in the book.

Direct experiences of nature enable us to enter fully into the spirit of the natural world. They help us discover a deep, inner sense of belonging and understanding. If people are to develop a love and concern for the earth, they need to have these direct experiences; otherwise, their knowing remains remote and theoretical and never touches them deeply.

After a deep, direct experience of nature, the mind is quiet and receptive, fully absorbed in the event. Direct experience awakens a sense of wonder. It enables us to reach out and feel other realities. With direct-experience learning, we stretch our awareness to include the surrounding world. Only with such empathy can we truly begin to *know* nature.

Thoreau said, "It is only by forgetting yourself that you draw near to God." This is just as true of nature. In the Stage 3 games, people expand beyond their own little worlds. They emerge from the narrow cocoon of self to discover a richer, larger world, filled with harmony.

STAGE 4:
SHARE INSPIRATION

"A joy shared is a joy doubled."

—Goethe

At the end of Stage 3, the players feel calmly exhilarated. They're now open to hearing stories that portray the noble ideals of the great naturalists, conservationists, and ecologists. They're in the right mood for activities that bring out nature's heart-warming, beautiful, and uplifting side.

Now is a good time, also, to let people talk about their earlier experiences while playing the games. Sharing reinforces the players' sense of wonder and draws the group together. The simple activities of the Inspiration stage also bring a sense of closure and wholeness to the day. The leader finds out what people have been thinking and feeling while they've played the games, and this stimulates lots of good ideas for leading future sessions.

The games and activities of the Inspiration stage are very simple. In Tree Imagery (page 98), for example, the players visualize themselves becoming a tree. They then experience the tree's life during one whole year's growth cycle. Tree Imagery ends with the players lying on their backs looking up through the branches of a deciduous tree. Having passed through the inwardness of winter and the renewal of spring, the group feels calm and energized.

After they've enjoyed lying on their backs watching the swaying branches, I ask the "trees" to sit up and express in three words, three phrases, or a single sentence what they've experienced during their year as a tree. Here are some of the statements people have made:

"I felt nourished by the sun, and felt I was giving back to the forest life around me."

"During the winter, my roots made me feel secure and unafraid, no matter how hard the wind blew."

"Vitality...a sense of community...renewal."

You could ask people to pantomime something they've seen or felt during your time together. They can act it out and have the others guess the meaning, then tell the meaning aloud if no one guesses correctly. If the group has become close and has experienced beautiful moments together, the sharings can be very powerful.

After leading a Flow Learning session, I sat at sundown with a group at the edge of a vast marsh. We watched the sunset for a long time, then did the pantomime activity just after the sun had gone down.

A twelve-year-old girl climbed to the top of the levee, turned toward us, and clasped her hands above her head, holding her arms in a circle. She stood there a moment smiling, then slowly walked backward down the other side of the levee. Her rendition of the sunset was so perfect that it touched everyone, reminding us of the beautiful moment we'd shared.

Often I've been amazed at how these sharings tend to bring out beautiful qualities in people. This was the case with one of the most challenging classes I've ever led. The group consisted of 30 English teenagers from a London inner-city slum. Some had fluorescent spiked hairdos. Others had safety pins stuck through their cheeks and slogans like "KILL" scrawled on the backs of their jackets.

I'd never before worked with a group quite like this one! I was surprised and pleased to see how even these hardened teenagers became caught up in the challenging, experiential Flow Learning games. At the end of the session, they seemed to have forgotten their tough, defiant roles, their cynical attitudes softened by feelings of connectedness and harmony which they'd received through the nature experiences.

In this case, it was very important to provide an opportunity for sharing. The teenagers told of their deep feelings of appreciation and concern for the earth. Their teacher said it had been a *long* time since she had seen them open their hearts and treat one another with respect.

You can end your outing with nature stories and tales from the lives of the great naturalists. I especially enjoy telling the story of Elzeard Bouffier from the book *The Man Who Planted Hope and Grew Happiness*, which recounts how one man single-handedly brought a dying land back to life. (This story is reprinted on page 142. See page 156 for other inspiring books about naturalists and conservationists.)

I also love to tell stories from the life of John Muir. You'll find stories from Muir's life especially powerful for inspiring people to live more idealistically. Children love to hear about Muir's exciting wilderness adventures and tender feeling for animals, while teenagers and adults also appreciate his personal philosophy and deep, mystical experiences of the unity of all life.

Summary

You don't have to confine the Flow Learning method to nature study—it's a wonderful tool for teaching many other subjects as well. The four stages will help you gauge student interest sensitively and structure your subject matter appropriately and creatively.

Let's say you're teaching a history class on the exploration of Africa. You can give your students wonderful "direct experiences" with a little help from the power of imagination. For a feeling of the vast tropical jungle, you might play African music softly in the background while you read from the journals of the early explorers. To awaken and focus the students' attention, you might have them listen to a tape of the tropical rain forest and count the many different animal sounds they hear.

I know a teacher who gets her children excited about learning about rain forests by closing the windows, turning on a heater and humidifier, and hanging plants everywhere to create a hot and steamy tropical environment. She then has the students look for pictures of camouflaged animals which she's hidden among the plants.

Teaching situations don't always allow full creative use of Flow Learning methods, but awareness of the stages can be valuable even when you use only a select few of them. For example, in a class on creative writing, to bring more vitality and richness of expression into the students' work, you could use imagination-stimulating exercises similar to those described above.

Let's say it's late afternoon, and everyone's feeling tired. To generate dynamic energy for learning, play some Stage 1 games to wake people up and lift their spirits. If the group becomes too rowdy, use some Stage 2 (Attention) activities to calm them down.

Good teachers are sensitive and flexible. Your success with Flow Learning will depend on how sensitively you respond to each group.

You must be able to change your plans when you see that something else will more effectively direct the students' interest and awareness to the next-higher level.

I recently talked with a woman who once worked as a naturalist at Grand Canyon National Park. She told me how frustrating it had been for her to try to convey the inspiration she felt from the Canyon to tourists who weren't all that interested. She said she'd always felt she was pulling them along by her own enthusiasm. The tourists got something out of her talks, but she wasn't satisfied, because she felt she was forcing her own ideas on them.

My naturalist friend felt her energy going out and not being returned. Her talks always left her drained. Good teaching is a dialogue, with people giving and receiving.

Sharing our inspiration with others verbally can take them part of the way. But to generate lasting, deep enthusiasm—for nature or any other subject—we must give others their own experiences. Enthusiasm for nature is always based on personal experience.

When I talked with my naturalist friend, I realized she'd been speaking about her feelings for the Canyon without taking the trouble to try to generate those same feelings in others by giving them direct experience. No wonder her audiences were unexcited and passive! She might have enjoyed her work much more if she had recognized the tourists' inexperience and often passive interest from the start. She could then have spent some time awakening their enthusiasm for the Canyon, focusing their attention, and setting the stage for some meaningful direct experiences. She could have concluded by sharing inspirational thoughts and stories.

The word "education" comes from the Greek for "to draw out or bring forth." When students can experience for themselves the knowledge we're trying to impart, their lessons become truly meaningful and are eagerly absorbed. Direct experience is as important in the classroom as it is outdoors.

Experiential learning isn't a new idea. What's unique about Flow Learning is that it lays out the stages a person goes through to get into a frame of mind where deep, direct experiences are possible. It's a tool to help people become receptive to nature as quickly and efficiently as possible. Because it's based on human nature, it can be creatively applied anywhere—in the classroom and in our personal lives.

STAGE 1: *Awaken Enthusiasm*

Quality: Playfulness & Alertness
Benefits:
- Builds on children's love of play.
- Creates an atmosphere of enthusiasm.
- A dynamic beginning gets everyone saying "Yes!"
- Develops full alertness, overcomes passivity.
- Creates involvement.
- Gets attention (minimizes discipline problems).
- Develops rapport with the leader.
- Creates good group dynamics.
- Provides direction and structure.
- Prepares for later, more sensitive activities.

STAGE 2: *Focus Attention*

Quality: Receptivity
Benefits:
- Increases attention span.
- Deepens awareness by focusing attention.
- Positively channels enthusiasm generated in Stage 1.
- Develops observational skills.

- Calms the mind.
- Develops receptivity for more sensitive nature experiences.

STAGE 3: *Direct Experience*

Quality: Absorption
Benefits:
- People learn best by personal discovery.
- Gives direct, experiential, intuitive understanding.
- Fosters wonder, empathy, and love.
- Develops personal commitment to ecological ideals.

STAGE 4: *Share Inspiration*

Quality: Idealism
Benefits:
- Clarifies and strengthens personal experiences.
- Builds on uplifted mood.
- Introduces inspiring role models.
- Gives peer reinforcement.
- Creates group bonding.
- Provides feedback for the leader.
- Leader can share inspiration with a receptive audience.

Chapter III

NATURE ACTIVITIES

This section gives games and
activities that illustrate the four stages
of Flow Learning. They
can be used
in Flow Learning sessions or
separately. To make it easy
to tell when a game will work best,
I've included a quick-reference
chart with each game.

QUICK-REFERENCE CHART FORMAT

A. An animal symbol indicates the appropriate stage for the activity:

STAGE 1: *Awaken Enthusiasm*
The otter spends his days frolicking. The only animal who plays—constantly!—throughout his adult life, he is nature's embodiment of exuberant fun.

STAGE 2: *Focus Attention*
The crow is an alert and intelligent creature, who keenly observes everything that goes on.

STAGE 3: *Direct Experience*
Bears are very curious by nature. Their solitary, quiet temperament also makes them a perfect symbol for direct experience.

STAGE 4: *Share Inspiration*
Dolphins are gregarious and altruistic creatures. They cooperate and care for one another, and they also appear to be conscious of other forms of life. There are many stories of drowning people being rescued by dolphins.

B. Concepts, attitudes and qualities taught by the game
C. When and where to play
D. Number of players needed
E. Best age range
F. Special materials, if any

In the Appendix, you'll find a list of all the activities from *Sharing Nature with Children* and *Sharing Nature with Children II*, arranged by stages. The list will help you plan your nature excursions.

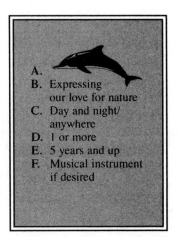
A.
B. Expressing our love for nature
C. Day and night/ anywhere
D. 1 or more
E. 5 years and up
F. Musical instrument if desired

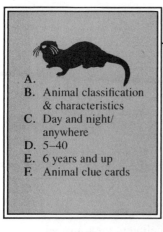

A.
B. Animal classification & characteristics
C. Day and night/ anywhere
D. 5–40
E. 6 years and up
F. Animal clue cards

As A BABY, I gain about nine pounds an hour. . . . When I'm resting, my pulse rate is 480 beats per minute. When I'm very active, it's 1280 beats per minute. . . . I have a lot of character for a guy without a backbone. . . . I am able to breathe and drink through my moist skin; I have two webbed feet. . . . When I'm born I look just like mom and dad—eight eyes and eight legs, and two body sections; our family doesn't have any wings or antennae. . . .

The Animal Clue Game is very good for capturing the group's enthusiasm at the start of a Flow Learning session. It breaks the ice and creates bonds between the people in the group.

Animal Clue requires a bit of preparation. You'll need forty 3×5 cards, on each of which you'll write a single clue to the identity of one of four animals (10 clue cards per animal). Once you're familiar with how the game works, you should feel free to vary the number of animals and clues.

To play, shuffle the clue cards and hand out one or two cards to each player. (It's okay to give each person clues to more than one animal.) The players should be standing so that they can mingle freely.

Tell the players that the goal of the game is to discover the identity of each of the four animals and gather all ten clue cards that

Animal
Clue
Game

describe each animal. Tell them not to begin until you give the signal, so that everyone can start together.

The players call out the names of the animals they think are described on their clue cards. A player's card might say: "You are warm-blooded and have a long tail and four feet." The player thinks, "Maybe I'm a squirrel," so he calls out, "Squirrel! Squirrel!" No one else shouts "Squirrel!", but someone is shouting "Otter!" and the player notices several other people heading in the Otter-person's direction. He checks his clue again and realizes he could be an otter, so he joins the group and they try to collect all ten otter clues.

For quickest results, the group should choose one person to try to collect all the otter clues. Similarly, they should assign one person to each of the other animals. Thus, a player might want to give his otter card to the otter collector and concentrate on his other cards.

The leader can mingle with the group, giving help as needed, but the players should rely on one another as much as possible. Children who can't read well or who are unfamiliar with the animals should be given the easiest clues.

Check each group's cards only when they say they've collected all ten clues. When all the animals are identified and the clue cards are gathered, have each group read two or three of their most interesting clues aloud.

Here are some hints for writing clues:

Unless you're working with experienced naturalists, choose animals with distinct and easily identified characteristics. For example, one is unlikely to confuse a bear with a snake while a bear and a raccoon are harder to distinguish. This also makes writing clues easier.

If a clue fits two animals, add a distinguishing characteristic. For example, if you're writing clues for a frog and a whale, the clue "I have to go to the surface to get air" is ambiguous, because it applies to both animals. Adding "...and I lay eggs." removes the ambiguity.

You can adapt the Animal Clue Game for use with very young children. Just make the clues simple and draw pictures on the cards. You might, for example, draw a round hole in a tree with the clue "This is my home," or draw a duck's feet with the clue "My feet look like this." For young players, use fewer animals and clues.

Sample Animal Clue Game:
You can use the following clues as given,
or simplify them for young children, or omit the easiest
clues for sophisticated players.

BLUE WHALE

- I'm the largest creature that ever lived on Earth. I'm bigger than three prehistoric dinosaurs and weigh as much as 35 African elephants.

- I can hear and talk with others of my kind over distances up to 35 miles. That's because sound travels better in water than in air. I also use "sonar"—like a bat.

- My body has a very thick layer of blubber (up to 2 feet thick during part of the year) which keeps me warm even in ice-cold ocean waters. With all that fat, I still look sleek and beautiful.

- I'm warm-blooded and feed my young milk. My young are born live—I don't lay eggs.

- I breathe through two holes in the top of my head. A relative of mine who has only one air-hole can hold his breath for an hour and a half and dive to ocean depths of 7,000 feet.

- Because of over-hunting, there are only six of us left for every hundred that used to live and swim in the ocean.

- My food is mostly a shrimp-like animal called krill. I eat about 3 tons of krill every day.

- Many animals came out of the sea to live on dry land—but I went back!

- As a baby I weigh 7 tons and am about 24 feet long. I gain 200 pounds every day—that's about 9 pounds an hour. When I'm three years old I'm up to 50 feet long.

- I can reach swimming speeds of 28 miles per hour for brief spurts.

HUMMINGBIRD

- I guard and protect "my" patch of flowers or garden. I may eat 50 to 60 meals there in a single day.

- Because of my bright and shiny colors, some names given to my kind in South and Central America are: shining sunbeam, red-tailed comet, white-bellied woodstar, purple-crowned fairy, and sunangel.

- I have two legs, hollow bones, and I'm warm-blooded.

- One of my kind is the smallest warm-blooded animal, just 2¼ inches long. I use up lots of energy. If humans expended as much energy per unit of weight as I do, they would have to eat 370 pounds of potatoes or 130 pounds of bread every day.

- When I'm resting, my pulse rate is 480 beats per minute. When I'm very active, it's 1280 beats per minute.

- My food is mainly nectar sipped from flowers, but I eat insects, too. I do not gather pollen.

- I can fly up, down, sideways, forward, backward, and hover motionless in the air. I achieve full flight speed almost instantly after takeoff.

- I usually lay 2 eggs that are pea-sized and white. My nest is an inch wide.

- I have a long beak and tiny feet.

- My wings move so fast they hum. I can beat my wings up to 79 times a second.

SPIDER

- Usually I'm brown, gray or black, but I can also be red, green or yellow. I do not have two or four legs, and really, I'm not such a bad fellow.

- I eat lots of insects, many of which carry diseases or are harmful to plants. I wear my skeleton on the outside of my body.

- I change my skin often as I grow older and larger. This process is called molting. I molt 4 to 12 times before I'm a full-grown adult. I never change my looks, just my size.

- Scorpions, ticks, mites, and crabs are some of my relatives.

- My eight simple eyes help me see to the front, behind, above, below, and to the sides. I also have eight legs.

- I have poison fangs to paralyze my prey. I suck out their insides and discard their empty shells.

- Most of us spin our own silk which we use to make egg cocoons, construct webs and traps, line our burrows, and wrap up our prey before we eat them.

- When I'm born I look just like Mom and Dad—eight eyes, two body sections, and quite a few legs. I don't have any wings or antennae, though.

- There are 50,000 species of my kind. We are very adaptable and live in many different places. Our kind have been around for 300 million years. Now many of us live with you in your house!

- I catch a lot of insects with a trap that I make.

FROG

- I am able to breathe and drink through my moist skin. I have two webbed feet.

- The males of my kind sing to attract the females. But neither males nor females build nests or care for our babies.

- I have four legs, two eyes, and a backbone.

- I'm green and live in and out of water.

- When I'm young I breathe water through gills. Later, as an adult, my body changes and I develop air-breathing lungs.

- My tongue is located at the tip of my mouth. I flip it out to catch insects.

- I'm cold-blooded, swim, and lay my eggs in water.

- If it's cold, I'll spend my winter in the mud on the bottom of a pond.

- I find safety in water from those who might try to eat me.

- When I'm young I eat plants, but as I grow older I change to a diet of insects.

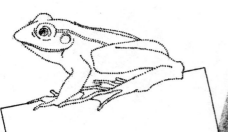

I am able to breathe and drink through my moist skin. I have two webbed feet.

I eat lots of insects, many of which carry diseases or are harmful to plants. I wear my skeleton on the outside of my body.

Natural
Processes

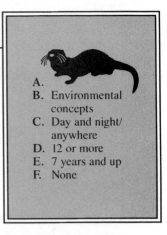

A.
B. Environmental concepts
C. Day and night/ anywhere
D. 12 or more
E. 7 years and up
F. None

I N THIS GAME, the group acts out a natural process such as plant succession, the water cycle, the food chain, or even glaciation and photosynthesis. Teachers and Scout leaders can use the game to review lessons they've taught earlier.

A good group size for Natural Processes is 12–18. With fewer than 12, there may not be enough players to take all the parts; with more than 20, some may feel left out. You can play Natural Processes with large groups by dividing them and giving each sub-group a different process to act. When the groups have prepared their "skits," call them together and have them take turns demonstrating their processes. Tell the audience not to guess aloud until a group has finished its performance.

To play Natural Processes, explain the game to the larger group, then divide it into smaller groups, if necessary. Meet with the small groups and assign them each a secret natural process. Set a time limit for preparing performances, and encourage the groups to be as creative as possible.

One group that was asked to demonstrate the water cycle assigned some of the members to play raindrops. The raindrops pantomimed falling from the sky, then rolled downhill to a make-believe lake while another player narrated the scenario in sign language.

In many of the games in this book, the players learn the principles of natural processes as they play. This is true to a certain extent for Natural Processes, but the game goes much more smoothly if the groups have one or more members who already understand the process you've assigned.

It's all right to use props, but not to the extent that they become the focus of the game and detract from a spirit of creative play and cooperation. Actions alone should tell the story—don't let the players fall back on explaining their concept with words. After the demonstration, the group can explain what they were doing, if they wish.

Build a Tree

THIS GAME HAS A MAGICAL POWER to create joyous camaraderie, as well as teach tree biology. It's amazingly effective for drawing a group together.

In Build a Tree, players act out the various parts of a tree: the taproot, lateral roots, heartwood, sapwood, phloem/cambium, and bark. In large groups, more than one player can take each role.

The heartwood section pantomimes providing strength and support for the tree. The roots (taproot and lateral) anchor the tree in the ground and draw up water and trace minerals. The sapwood carries water up to the branches and leaves. The cambium is the growing part of the tree. The phloem carries food from the leaves to the rest of the tree, and the bark protects the tree.

HEARTWOOD: To begin play, choose two or three tall, strong-looking people and ask them to play the heartwood. Have them stand with their backs to each other. Tell the rest of the group, "This is the heartwood—the inner core, the strength of the tree. The heartwood's job is to hold the trunk and branches upright so the leaves can get their share of the sun. The heartwood has been around a long time—so long that it's dead; but it's well preserved! The heartwood used to be alive, but its thousands of little tubes that carried water up and food down are now all clogged with resin and pitch." Tell the heartwood players that their job is to "stand tall and strong."

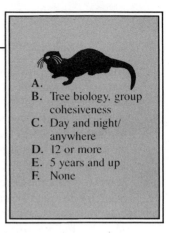

A.
B. Tree biology, group cohesiveness
C. Day and night/ anywhere
D. 12 or more
E. 5 years and up
F. None

TAPROOT: Next, ask several people to play the taproot. Tell them to sit down at the base of the heartwood, facing outward. Tell them: "You are a very long root, called a taproot. Plant yourself deep in the ground—about thirty feet. The taproot enables the tree to get water from deep in the earth, and also anchors the tree firmly to the ground. When storms come, the taproot keeps the tree from being blown over by high winds." Be sure to say that not all trees have a taproot (e.g., redwoods), but that this one does.

LATERAL ROOTS: Choose people with long hair who look as if they won't mind lying on the ground. Ask the "lateral roots" to lie on their backs with their feet up against the trunk and their bodies extending away from the tree. Tell them: "You are the lateral roots. There are hundreds and hundreds of you. You grow outward all around the tree, like branches but underground. You also help hold the tree upright. At your tips are tiny root hairs."

At this point, kneel beside one of the lateral roots and spread his hair out around his head. Continue your narrative: "Trees have thousands of miles of root hairs that cover every square inch of soil into which they grow. When they sense that there is water nearby, the cells grow toward it and suck it up. The tips of the root hairs have cells as tough as football helmets. I want the lateral roots and taproot to practice slurping up water. When I say 'Let's slurp!' you all go like this. (Make a loud slurping noise.) Okay, let's hear you slurp!"

SAPWOOD: Now ask a small group to play the sapwood. Choose enough people to form a complete circle around the heartwood. Have them circle the heartwood, facing inward and holding hands, being careful not to step on any roots! Tell them: "You are the part of the tree called the sapwood, or xylem. You draw water up from the roots and lift it to the tree's highest branches. You are the most efficient pump in the world, with no moving parts. You're able to lift hundreds of gallons of water a day, and you do this at speeds of over 100 miles an hour! After the roots slurp the water from the ground, your job is to bring the water up the tree. When I say 'Bring the water up!', you go like this: 'Wheeee!' (As they do this, they throw their arms up into the air.) Let's practice. First we'll have the roots slurp. Let's slurp!" Follow this immediately by commanding the sapwood, "Bring the water up! Wheeee!"

CAMBIUM/PHLOEM: Select a group to play the cambium/phloem. Have them form a circle around the sapwood, also facing inward and holding hands. Tell them: "Toward the inside of the tree from you is the cambium layer, the growing part of the tree. Every year it adds a new layer to the sapwood and phloem. A tree grows outward from its trunk, and also from the tips of its roots and branches. It doesn't grow like your hair does." (Push the fingers of one hand upward through the horizontal fingers of the other hand.)

"Behind you, toward the outside of the tree, is the phloem. This is the part of the tree that carries food manufactured by the leaves and distributes it to the rest of the tree. Let's turn our hands into leaves."

Have them stretch their arms upward and outward so that they intersect each other's arms at wrists and forearms, leaving their hands free to flutter like leaves.

"When I say 'Let's make food!' raise your arms and flutter your leaves and absorb the energy from the sun and make food. And when I say 'Bring the food down', you go 'Whoooo!' " (Make the 'Whoooo!' a long, descending sound while you bend at the knees and drop your arms and body toward the ground.) "Let's practice."

Go through all the sounds and motions with all the parts, in this order: "Let's slurp!" "Let's make food!" "Bring the water up!" "Bring the food down!" (Notice that the cambium/phloem ring makes food before the sapwood brings the water up. Make sure also that they don't raise their arms and flutter their leaves until you say "Let's make food." This way their arms won't get tired.)

Ask the remaining people to play the bark. Have them circle round

the tree, facing outward. Tell them: "You are the bark. What kind of dangers do you protect the tree from?"

Suggest fire, insects, extreme temperature changes, and little boys and girls with pocket knives. Tell the bark how they protect the tree: "Raise your arms like a football blocker with both elbows out and both fists close to the chest. (Pause) Do you hear that high-pitched sound? It's a feisty and very hungry long-snouted pine-borer. I'll go and see if I can stop it. If I don't come back, you'll have to stop the pine-borer yourselves."

Disappear behind a tree and come out as the pine-borer. Ham it up by scowling, using branches for your antennae, and turning your head back and forth. Zero in with your antennae and point your long borer-snout toward the tree. Now run or walk quickly around the tree, pretending to try to penetrate the bark's protective layer. The "bark" people should try to fend you off.

While you are going around the tree, lead the rest of the tree groups in their parts. Shout the commands for all the parts in sequence. Go through the sequence three or four times. The commands for the tree parts are as follows:

Nature Activities 65

(First time only) "Heartwood, stand tall and strong!" and "Get tough, Bark!" 1) "Roots, let's slurp!" 2) "Leaves, let's make food!" 3) "Sapwood, bring the water up!" 4) "Phloem, bring the food down!"

After the first round, just shout the commands without giving the names of the tree parts. When you finish, have the players give themselves a big hand for being such a wonderful tree. And help the roots up off the ground!

Nature Bingo

DURING THE TIME I worked as a naturalist at Glacial Trails Scout Ranch in the high Sierras, almost every August a storm would blow in, bringing three or four days of hard rain. Hundreds of little streams ran wild through the campsites, and by the second day of the deluge, the Scouts' belongings were completely soaked. One by one, they gratefully left their drenched and sagging tents and crammed themselves into the camp's few buildings.

During these storms, there wasn't much interest in outdoor programs, but the Scouts needed something to do, so I tried to think up a game that would be meaningful as well as entertaining. Nature Bingo turned out to be the perfect choice.

Nature Bingo is played just like regular bingo, but using objects from nature instead of numbers.

To make the game more entertaining, we played it like a TV game

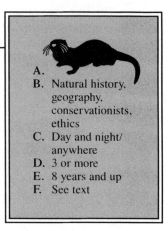

A.
B. Natural history, geography, conservationists, ethics
C. Day and night/ anywhere
D. 3 or more
E. 8 years and up
F. See text

show, complete with ludicrous prizes. One of my favorite prizes was the 2:00 a.m. guided owl hike. Other prizes that drew lots of comment, though not much enthusiasm from the winners, were the triple-decker peanut butter and lard sandwich, and the holiday-for-two package tour inviting you and a buddy to the tropical warmth of the kitchen for cleanup chores. There were always a sufficient number of real prizes to encourage the boys to participate, and they roared with delight when their friends won the more ludicrous offerings. We played for hours, and the game helped immensely to keep the Scouts' spirits up during rainy spells.

For an added twist, we would hide three prizes under large bowls. The winner could choose a can of food with the label torn off, or take his chances on one of the hidden prizes. Every Scout had his own idea about which bowl hid the most desirable prize, and they didn't hesitate to make their opinions known. Shouts of "Two!", "No— Three!"and "One! One!" filled the air.

What held the Scouts' interest, apart from the prizes, was the new and interesting information the game gave. To play Nature Bingo, you need to create five category headings for nature-subjects. The categories I chose for the sample card in this book are: Endangered Species, Plants & Animals, Ecology Concepts, Natural Places, and Conservationists. Each category should have at least 8–10 subjects. For example, the Conservationists heading might have a card listing five of the following subjects: Aldo Leopold, Saint Francis, Mary Austin, Richard St. Barbe Baker, John Muir, John Wesley Powell, Rachel Carson, and Chief Seattle. Make enough cards to equal the number of players. Each card should be unique.

You'll also need to make a tab for each subject. On the tab, write the subject and the heading. See the sample bingo card for the five category headings and examples of subjects for each category. Pass the cards around, and tell the players that you'll draw one of the tabs and call out the heading first, then the subject. For example: "Natural Places. . . . Tallgrass Prairie." The players mark their cards with beans, pebbles, etc., and the player who covers five places in a row first wins. The winner, of course, calls out "Bingo!" Players can win with five subjects in a row vertically, horizontally, or diagonally.

Have the winning player call out his five items, to double-check that all the subjects have been called. If you place the subject tabs in their respective columns while you read them, it'll be easier to locate subjects when you check the winning player's card. To add to the learning experience, you can call out the heading, then before calling out the subject, tell a story or give interesting information about the subject. For example, for the Endangered Species heading, you could say, "Because of over-hunting, there are only six of us left for every hundred that formerly swam in the ocean." The players then try to guess the subject of the story (in this case, blue whales). Or you might say, "This bird has a five-foot-long windpipe shaped like the coiled tubes of a trumpet. When disturbed or angry, or when threatening intruders, it gives a ringing call that can be heard for several miles: Ker-loo! ker-loo!" (Whooping Crane)

The Conservationist category is especially good for sharing the inspiring thoughts of men and women who've spoken eloquently for the earth. For example: "Like winds and sunsets, wild things were taken for granted until progress began to do away with them. Now we must face the question whether a still higher standard of living is worth its cost in things natural, wild, and free." (Aldo Leopold) Or, "Every part of this Earth is sacred to my people. Every shining pine needle, every sandy shore, every mist in the dark woods, every clearing and humming insect is holy in the memory and experience of my people." (Chief Seattle)

For the Natural Places category, you could say: "The walls of the valley are made up of rocks, mountainous in size. . . . [It] is about seven miles long, half a mile to a mile wide, and nearly a mile deep. . . . Every rock in its walls seems to glow with life . . . [and] the crystal Merced—river of mercy—peacefully glides through its meadows." (Yosemite Valley, described by John Muir)

Let the players think for a few seconds, then ask them to guess aloud. If they're stumped, give the correct answer.

You can involve the players more by having them create the clues, perhaps dividing them into groups, one group per category.

Nature Bingo Sample Card

ENDANGERED SPECIES	PLANTS & ANIMALS	ECOLOGY CONCEPTS	NATURAL PLACES	CONSERVATIONISTS
Cacti	Sea Squirt	Symbiosis	Serengeti Plain	Rachel Carson
		Niche	Amaz... Basi...	
Mountain Gorilla	Grunt			
	Baby Blue Eyes	Ecology	Grand Canyon	
Wolf	Fairy Ring	Mimicry		Henry David Thoreau

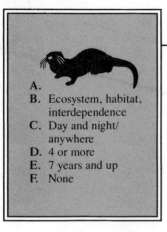

A.
B. Ecosystem, habitat, interdependence
C. Day and night/anywhere
D. 4 or more
E. 7 years and up
F. None

IN THIS GAME, five players—ideally, volunteers—"create" a natural environment. Each player chooses to play one of the environment's components, such as a plant, animal, or physical feature. Children who play the game quickly learn to associate plants and animals with their particular environments. The Habitat Game also makes it easy for them to understand how various elements cooperate to form communities of living and nonliving things, each interacting with the others. The camaraderie of the game also helps bond the group together.

After choosing a group of five players, secretly tell the group the environment they'll play. Without prior discussion, have the players choose their component of the environment and immediately begin playing their roles. While each group performs, the people in the larger group watch, refraining from guessing the environment until the performers have finished their "act."

Let's say you've asked a group to play the ocean beach environment. One player may choose to run back and forth, playing waves crashing on the beach. The second player may run in and out just beyond the reach of the waves, bobbing and poking his head up and down like a sandpiper. The third player may crouch and walk sideways—a crab, he's hiding from the fourth player who's chosen to play a sea gull. Many roles remain for the fifth player to choose from: sunbather, clam, sea palm, starfish, and so on.

After the players have been performing for a while, ask the audience which environment is being portrayed. Before the players leave the "stage," have each introduce the character he's played, in order of appearance. Encourage the rest of the group to express their appreciation by applauding the actors.

Other environments that are easy to act are: forest, meadow, mountain, and desert. It's all right to let the players choose their own environments, but don't let the group discuss each player's role, or they'll take too much time and keep the larger group waiting. If you decide to allow time for the group to discuss and plan their "act," first divide the larger group into smaller teams so that they can all work on their environments simultaneously.

Habitat

Getting Acquainted

THIS ACTIVITY was designed by Cliff Knapp, author of *Humanizing Environmental Education*, to help people get to know one another better. After playing the game, groups almost always feel more relaxed and work together better.

To play the game, pass out sheets of paper on which you've printed the items listed below. (Feel free to make up your own list.) Each player must interview the other people in the group, asking questions and marking the items with the names of people who meet the listed criteria. Tell them to try to get each person's name on the list at least once, but not to linger too long with any one person.

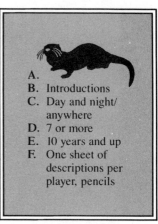

A.
B. Introductions
C. Day and night/ anywhere
D. 7 or more
E. 10 years and up
F. One sheet of descriptions per player, pencils

THE GETTING ACQUAINTED QUESTIONNAIRE

Find someone who:
- Claims prairie roots: _____
- Has a hero in the conservation or natural history field: _____
  Name of Hero: _____
- Sits quietly every day and observes nature: _____
- Has written a letter to a government official about an environmental issue: _____
- Has seen an endangered species: _____ Species: _____
- Knows who John Wesley Powell is: _____
- Knows a good story about how the stars were created: _____
- Has slept in a tipi: _____
- Has helped an injured animal or tree: _____
- Has an exciting or inspiring nature experience to tell: _____
- If he were to turn into a plant or animal, has a favorite plant or animal he'd like to be: _____
  Favorite plant or animal: _____
- Can recite a poem, song, or quotation about nature: _____
- Has a favorite outdoor activity: _____
- Has gotten lost outdoors: _____
- Has lived without electricity for an extended period of time: _____
- Has overcome a personal limitation while in nature: _____
- Has seen at least one of the following animals in the wild: scissor-tailed flycatcher, backswimmer, giraffe, California sister, bobcat, gannet, or humpback whale: _____
- Can name three books he would like to have with him, if stranded on a deserted island: _____
  Names of books: _____ , _____ , _____ .

Nature Activities

THE DRUMMING *of a woodpecker. Wind rushing and roaring through the tree tops. The flute-like call of a hermit thrush. The "buzz" from a nearby hummingbird. Water cascading and singing down a steep, rocky incline.*

A thrilling chorus of natural sounds delights the players in the Sound Map Game. Children love this activity—they become completely absorbed and sit surprisingly still while making their sound maps.

To play, begin by showing the group a 4 × 6 index card with an X in the center. Tell the players the card is a map, and that the X shows where they're sitting. When they hear a sound, they should make a mark on the card that aptly describes the sound. The mark's location should indicate as accurately as possible the direction and distance of the sound. The marks should be interpretive, not literal: the players don't have to draw pictures of plants and animals, just a few lines that represent the sound—for example, two wavy lines indicating wind, or a musical note indicating a songbird. In other words, they should spend little time drawing and most of the time listening.

Tell the players to keep their eyes closed while they listen. Explain that cupping their hands behind their ears provides a reflective surface for catching sounds, creating a shape like the sensitive ears of a fox or kangaroo. To hear sounds behind them, they needn't turn their heads, but just cup their hands in front of their ears.

Select a site where the group is likely to hear a variety of sounds—meadows, streams, and forests are fine. It's important to have everyone find a special "listening place" quickly, so that some aren't walking around while others are already listening. I usually give the group one minute to find a spot and tell them to stay in the same spot until the end of the game. Giving the players enough time to disperse fairly widely will ensure a diversity of sound maps and greater interest in sharing.

How long you should play depends on the group's age, attention span, and how well-supplied the environment is with sounds. A good basic guideline is 10 minutes for adults, 5–10 minutes for children. I like to call the group back together by imitating a natural sound or

A.
B. Auditory awareness, calmness
C. Day and night/natural area
D. 1 or more
E. 5 years and up
F. Index card and pencil per player

Sound Map

blowing a crow or duck call. As the players assemble, ask them to share their maps with a partner.

It's sometimes hard to find a site that's protected from the sounds of cars and machinery, but these noisy areas are ideal for teaching lessons about noise pollution. Have the children make two sound maps, the first one near a busy street and the second in a quiet, natural spot. After the game, ask them where they felt more comfortable. This is a fine way to build children's conscious appreciation of natural areas.

After the children have drawn their maps and shared them, you can ask questions such as:

- How many different sounds did you hear?
- Which sounds did you like best? Why?
- Which sounds did you like least? Why?
- Which sounds had you never heard before? Do you know what made the sounds?

Instead of having them answer aloud, you can ask them to circle the sounds they'd never heard before, draw one line under sounds they liked best and two lines under the sounds they liked least.

Nature Activities

Wilderness Trail

AT THE Woodleaf Outdoor Education Program, where I worked some years ago, we taught many large classes of sixth-graders. To give each student the experience of being completely alone in nature, we designed an activity called Wilderness Trail.

We told the children that Native Americans of their age would go out into the wilderness alone to seek wisdom from nature, because they felt that if you were quiet and attentive, Nature could teach you a great deal about life and about yourself.

We gave the children binoculars, magnifying glasses, and other instruments to keep them busy and interested, but we emphasized that the most important thing was to sit completely still and become sensitively aware of their surroundings.

It's very important that the children be spaced evenly along the trail, out of sight of one another. Here's a good way to accomplish this: When you come to a beautiful place on the trail, raise your hand. Children who want that spot *silently* raise their hands, and the first child to do so is chosen. This way, the children have some say in where they'll sit, without disturbing the silent, reflective mood.

To separate "lively" pairs of students: Let's imagine that Jay and Danny have a proven talent for synthesizing mischief. You've just left Jay, and when you come to the next spot Danny already has his hand up. The solution? Simple—choose the student behind Danny!

It helps to leave behind a second leader who starts walking along the trail after a prearranged interval (20–30 minutes works well), collecting the children. Encourage the players to remain quiet during the walk back. When the group has regathered, the mood will usually be right for some sharing activities, so try to end at a spot where the group can sit comfortably.

If the players have never been alone in nature, playing Sound Map and Path of Knowledge first will help allay their nervousness. When they're feeling more at ease outdoors, you can try Wilderness Trail.

A.
B. Solitude, wildlife observation
C. Day/any natural area
D. 1–35
E. 8 years and up
F. None

Barefoot
Walk

"I'VE BEEN in such a hurry all my life, I've never taken the time to notice nature," a friend confessed one day. I had often watched her marching determinedly, head down, on the footpaths near our home, oblivious of ponderosa pines, billowing clouds, and brilliant blue sky.

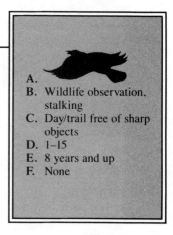

A.
B. Wildlife observation, stalking
C. Day/trail free of sharp objects
D. 1–15
E. 8 years and up
F. None

All of us get caught up in thinking about the future and planning our lives, to the extent that we sometimes overlook what the present moment has to offer. A fine way to encourage people to slow down is to take them on a barefoot walk. It's amazing how quiet and attentive even large groups become when they have to pay attention to where they're putting their feet!

The barefoot walk is also one of the best ways I know to observe wildlife. On numerous barefoot walks, groups I've led have come close to animals such as coyotes and foxes which were caught unawares by our silent approach. I once walked barefoot into the middle of a covey of quail. One quail spotted me and gave the alarm, and then they all scurried into the brush, clucking "whit-whit-whit." Some, not knowing where the danger lay, ran close by me.

Just a few feet up the trail on that same walk, I stood by a small tree while a flock of lesser goldfinches swooped into the nearby branches. Their yellow, black and green bodies decorated the tree like Christmas ornaments. I stood as quietly as possible while I watched them from a few feet away.

There is a wonderful quality to the experience of watching animals close-up in the wild, entering into their world quietly and unobtrusively. There's none of the panic that accompanies the usual noisy human intrusion into their habitat. Wild animals going about their activities are serene and poised. Watching them stimulates feelings of kinship with the animal world.

A slow pace encourages the walkers to pause and look around, increasing their chances of seeing wildlife. If you schedule the hike for sunrise or sunset, more animals will be moving about. The calm, reflective atmosphere at dawn and dusk helps the group tune in to the spirit of quiet observation.

An entertaining way to introduce the game is to teach the players to walk quietly, Indian-fashion. Ask them to take off their shoes and socks. Then have them take a very slow, *short* step forward, coming down gently on the outside of the descending foot and rolling it inward slowly until the foot is level. At this point, the sole of the foot should be only lightly touching the ground. Before shifting full weight onto the lead foot, they should feel whether there are any twigs, leaves, or other objects that might make a noise. If there aren't, tell them to bring their weight slowly onto the lead foot. Tell them that by taking short steps they'll have better balance and thus will feel free to give more attention to looking for animals.

After learning to walk quietly, people are eager to try out their new skill—the idea of taking one's shoes off and walking barefoot seems perfectly natural! (Be sure to check the area for glass, stickers, and sharp gravel.)

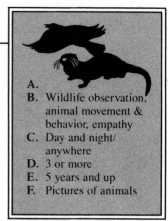

A.
B. Wildlife observation,
   animal movement &
   behavior, empathy
C. Day and night/
   anywhere
D. 3 or more
E. 5 years and up
F. Pictures of animals

Animals, Animals!

T HE COMPUTER ANALYST *curled up in front of us and yawned. As our group of forty watched, she carefully lifted her left hand to her mouth, licked the back of her hand and gently rubbed it against her cheek. Instantly, we knew she was a cat. She then crouched low, her entire body tensed and alert. She sprang forward and pounced on an invisible prey. "Mountain lion!" we called out, amid laughter and applause.*

Animals, Animals! is a good game for helping people develop deeper rapport with animals. There are two ways to play the game. The first version, using animal pictures, is playful and makes a good beginning for an outdoor session. The second is more serious, often profound, and creates great empathy through observation of live animals.

ANIMALS, ANIMALS! VERSION 1

This version can be played with all kinds of hilarious variations. It always draws a group together in a spirit of fun and creates many opportunities for spontaneous discussion of natural history concepts.

To begin, explain that you'll pass out animal picture cards and that

---

Nature Activities   81

the players should keep "their" animal's identity secret. After you pass out the cards, have the players act out their animals' typical behavior, one "actor" at a time.

If you have a large group, you might want to ask for 8 or 10 volunteers to "perform" for the others. In such a situation, you can place a variety of picture cards on the ground and let each player choose the animal he feels best able to imitate.

When an "animal" comes "on stage," tell him to visualize his animal in his mind first, then capture the animal's essence in a still pose. After he's held the pose for eight seconds, tell him to move around like the animal. To end his performance, he can, if he wishes, make the animal's sounds, warbling, braying, and so on.

The other players guess what the animal is. It's very important to let the player finish his "act" before calling out names. To help the group restrain their eagerness, tell them you'll wave an arm when it's time to start guessing. If a player can't mimic his animal's call very well, or if he quickly runs out of movements, let everyone begin guessing a bit sooner.

It's all right to give clues, if you have to, but you'll be surprised by the wonderful imitations most players come up with. Someone nearly always guesses what the animal is very quickly.

In most games that require a performance, it adds to the fun to designate an area as the "stage" and have each player come forward to perform, rather than do his act wherever he is standing. Before each performance, ask the player to give you his card, so you know what animal he is and can help the audience with hints, if need be.

The animals you choose should be easily identifiable, with well-known physical characteristics and movements. Some perennial favorites are: bear, bat, penguin, gorilla, turtle, owl, leopard, and heron.

ANIMALS, ANIMALS! VERSION 2

If you play Animals, Animals! at a zoo, farm, or wilderness area, be sure to take advantage of opportunities to let the players see real, live animals. If you tell the group you're going to ask them to play the animals later, it'll whet their interest in observing them closely. They'll learn more, and it'll also increase their empathy for "their" animal.

If the players are old enough, send them out alone to look for an

animal they find especially interesting. If some of the players feel unsure of themselves outdoors, or if they're new to nature games, send them out in teams of three.

I remind the players that dragonflies, lizards, and butterflies are animals, too, and that they're much easier to observe than bobcats or eagles. Some groups have a hard time relating to small animals like insects. But if there aren't any large animals in the area, you could give the players a choice of imitating other natural phenomena, such as grass, rocks, and trees.

Tell the players to observe the animal's movements, sounds, rhythms, and physical characteristics carefully. If they're inclined, they can also silently ask the animal to reveal its inner essence and beauty.

Tell the players that after they've observed their animals, they should imagine they *are* the animal and try to move and think like it. Tell them this is a perfect time to practice their "act," because they'll be alone and able to study the animal in real life. Feeling a close bond with the animal will make it easier to act their role convincingly.

Before sending the players out, you might want to play Animals, Animals! with pictures. I've found that when I do this, the players are much more enthusiastic about Version 2.

A wonderful way to introduce the spirit of Animals, Animals! is to read aloud from *Another Way to Listen*, by Byrd Baylor and Peter Parnall. (See the recommended reading at the end of the book.)

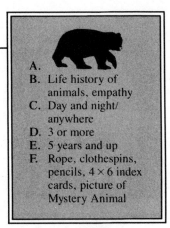

A.
B. Life history of animals, empathy
C. Day and night/ anywhere
D. 3 or more
E. 5 years and up
F. Rope, clothespins, pencils, 4 × 6 index cards, picture of Mystery Animal

Mystery Animal

YEARS AGO, I was wandering with a friend in the fields near my home when I saw a beautiful bird about the size of a robin, but smaller and thinner. Neither of us had ever seen such a strikingly-colored bird. Its head and back were black, its eyes were brilliant red, its sides were chestnut-colored, and its belly was white. Its back and wings were covered with dazzling white spots. When it flew, there was a flashing display of browns, whites, and blacks. We didn't know anyone who could tell us the bird's name, nor did we have the trained eyes of a bird watcher, so we didn't have any luck picking it out from the hundreds of pictures in a bird book.

Every day for two weeks, I went out to look at these birds. I discovered that they fed on the ground by pulling up leaves and twigs to uncover seeds and insects. They scratched in the leaves so vigorously that they made more noise than a deer. (Another friend called them "masters of the double-footed scratch.") They gave a trilling call, and also a cat-like "meow." For me, these birds seemed marvelous and mysterious.

My interest in birds grew into curiosity about all living things. The experience of not receiving quick answers also taught me a valuable lesson: I realized that no matter what the subject was, the longer my curiosity burned, the more I learned. Applied to nature study, this means that people learn far more deeply when they're captivated by a sense of mystery.

By the way, the bird was a rufous-sided towhee, western race.

In Mystery Animal, the leader shares intriguing information about an animal without giving its name. To play, the group should be seated comfortably, near enough to hear you clearly. Tell them you're going to take them on a trip to see a very unusual animal. Urge them to pay close attention to everything they "see," because they'll have

People are eagerly looking at a photograph of the Mystery Animal.

to create a "field report" on the animal and its environment afterwards.

To give your narrative the power of a guided visualization, use descriptions that involve the senses: jungle noises, tropical heat and humidity, the smell of forest greenery and rotting leaves, and so on. Include as much humor as you like.

The following example narrative is just about the right length to hold the interest of adults and teenagers. With younger children, you'll probably need to shorten it. I've found it's more dynamic to memorize some of the most important points and narrate the imagery extemporaneously, instead of reading from a script.

When you finish, pass out pencils and 4×6 cards. Tell the players that their field report should be a picture of the animal in its environment. (Many people are self-conscious about their inability to draw, so I never mention drawing until this point. And to lessen their discomfort, I tell them they don't need to sign their reports.)

While they draw, tie a light rope or heavy string between two trees or branches. When they're finished, ask the group to attach their pictures with clothespins to the line for an informal "art exhibit." There'll be lots of discussion and laughter as the players scrutinize one another's drawings. Finally, ask them if they'd like to see a photograph of the animal.

The players' enthusiasm will amaze you. Faces glow with concentration as they search the photograph for details you've mentioned and for details they've included in their drawings.

Mystery Animal works very well with young children, especially on a field trip to the zoo. Before taking the children around the zoo to see the animals, gather them together and introduce the game. Describe a mystery animal and tell them to let you know if they see the animal. (Make the Mystery Animal one of your last stops.) Watching little children look intently at each animal, trying to discover whether it's the mystery animal, is very touching.

With children too young to draw the animal, you can set up 6–8 pictures of different animals and ask the children to choose the right one.

Mystery Animal provides a fine excuse to tell about animals whose stories seldom get told—an environmentally threatened butterfly whose life history isn't well known, for example.

With older children, you can ask the players to create their own Mystery Animal stories and then share them with the group.

A SAMPLE MYSTERY ANIMAL STORY

You are in one of the last great unexplored regions on earth. Charles Darwin called it "one great, wild, luxuriant hothouse." The temperature is nearly always over 80 degrees Fahrenheit, the humidity is 80%, and the average annual rainfall is over 13 feet (156 inches). Because of these favorable conditions, the tropical rain forest harbors a greater variety of life than any other environment on earth. Look high above you. You see a thick canopy of branches. Only 1% of the sunlight ever reaches the forest floor, so few plants cover the ground, and walking is easy. You begin to walk through the forest. You see strange plants around you. You hear a chorus of wild, shrieking, croaking, and clicking cries: monkeys, birds, frogs, and insects. You smell rotting vegetation.

High above, hanging under a branch, you see something move. It looks like a mass of dead leaves, moldy fungus, or a termite's nest. But, look—it moved again! Use your binoculars to get a closer look. Yes, it's an animal, and it's hanging upside down from a branch. It has long, coarse hair and four long limbs. Each foot has claws that look like bailing hooks. It is about two feet long and seems to weigh around 14 pounds. Its rounded head is no bigger than its neck, and it doesn't have any ears that you can see. It's very hard to tell which end is the front and which is the rear, because you can't see a tail. Aha! Its face is turning toward you. Study it closely. Its face is flat and whitish, and its mouth makes it look like it's always smiling.

This animal isn't known for its speed; in fact, it moves like a slow-motion movie. Amoebas are said to stream faster than this animal moves. It's beginning to move now. See why it moves so slowly . . . (pause) . . . it's moving just one limb at a time. See it reach slowly for the branch nearest to it. It's almost got it. (Pause) There! Now watch its other leg begin to move. It may take half a minute to shift its legs only a few inches. One mother who was hurrying toward her baby 15 feet away covered the distance in just over an hour. Its extreme slowness makes it hard to see by its main enemies: jaguars and harpy eagles. Its top speed in the trees is a little over 1 mph, but on land it's only 1/10 mph. This is because its legs can't support it, so it has to drag itself along the ground. It doesn't come down out of the trees very often—only to give birth and to go to the bathroom. The latter occurs infrequently—once every seven or eight days.

After following and studying this animal in the jungle for a week, a scientist jokingly remarked that some people might say it had an ideal life, because this is how it spent its time:

    11 hours feeding
    18 hours just moving slowly about
    10 hours resting
    129 hours sleeping

It spent 18 out of every 24 hours sleeping! Its metabolism is also very slow—these animals have been known not to need to breathe for as long as thirty minutes while under water.

It doesn't spend much time on personal hygiene, and it doesn't clean its fur. As many as 978 beetles were found living in the fur of one individual. In fact, nine species of moths, four species of beetles, six species of ticks, and several species of mites have been found living happily together in its hair.

During the rainy season, algae grows on its fur. The greenish tint of the algae serves as camouflage. Caterpillars feed on its moldy hair, then pupate and fly away as moths.

This animal seems so primitive and slow-witted that you wonder how it has managed to escape extinction. Its success is due to several factors: protective coloration, the habit of feeding mostly at night and remaining motionless during the day, and its twenty-three pairs of ribs, (humans have twelve), heavy coating of fur, and thick, tough skin, all of which protect its internal organs. "Of all animals," wrote Charles Waterton, "this poor, ill-formed creature is the most tenacious of life." It has the ability to survive wounds that would kill any other animal. Although many people make fun of this animal, it has been said that no other creature is better adapted to life in the tropical rain forest.

The animal we've been observing hasn't moved in quite a while and is now doing what it does best: sleeping. Before we head back to camp, let's take one more good look with our binoculars. Notice its bear-like body, its coarse hair hanging down toward its back, and its long limbs, each with three long, curved claws.

The Mystery Animal is a three-toed sloth. It lives in the tropical forests of South and Central America. There's a picture of a sloth on page 159.

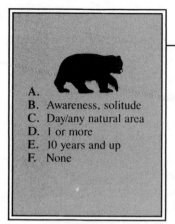

A.
B. Awareness, solitude
C. Day/any natural area
D. 1 or more
E. 10 years and up
F. None

PATH OF KNOWLEDGE gives the players a direct experience of one aspect of nature. They walk along a path spread out, single-file, looking for something that is particularly beautiful or meaningful to them. They may feel drawn to an old tree, a tumbling stream, or a brightly-colored flower. Whatever attracts them, encourage them to stop and try to feel its essential qualities. Ask them to think of a word or brief phrase that describes their discovery. When everyone has walked the trail, have the players give their descriptions.

Before walking The Path of Knowledge, the players should be in a quiet, observant mood, so it's best to save this game for Stage 3. If you can, choose a wooded trail where the group can spread out, so that each person feels alone. If the trail twists and turns, you can shorten the interval between players. This will spare those near the back from having to wait very long. With a large group, you can lead quiet activities for those who're waiting their turn. Choose a trail that has lots of interesting features.

We played Path of Knowledge at a winter workshop in Iowa, where we walked through a beautiful forest and prairie and emerged at a pond. On the way in, everyone was deeply absorbed in the beautiful winter landscape, but on the way back, because we had to get back quickly, I let the group amble along without any planned activity. The difference was amazing: Everyone was talking, and I think no one was even remotely aware of the beautiful surroundings. The teachers had been out all day, and it was natural for them to want to relax and visit, but it was a valuable demonstration of how structured activities focus attention and heighten awareness of nature.

You can simplify this activity by giving the children photographs of settings or features that are visible from the trail, then have each child walk the Path of Knowledge trail looking for the subject of his photograph. Special trees, distinctive rocks, and striking scenes are all good choices.

Path of Knowledge

Guided Imagery

A.
B. Intuitive appreciation, concentration, empathy
C. Day or night/anywhere
D. 2 or more
E. 5 years and up
F. If done with music: cassette player & tape

L

ONG BEFORE

the sun came, they were making ready for flight.
When the drafts were complete, there came a faint tone of
excitement into their speech. They began moving
their heads from side to side in
jerks. And then, turning into the wind,
suddenly they would all be in the air together,
fourteen or forty at a time, with wide wings scooping
the blackness and a cry of triumph in their
throats. They would wheel round, climbing
rapidly, and be gone from sight.
Arthur began to feel an uneasiness in himself.
He became restless. . . . He wanted to join in, and to
enjoy the exercise of morning flight, which was
so evidently a pleasure. They
had a comradeship, free discipline and
joie de vivre. *When the goose next to him spread*
her wings and leaped, he did so automatically.

—FROM THE ONCE AND FUTURE KING
BY T. H. WHITE

Legend tells us that when King Arthur was a boy, he was taught by Merlin, the great magician. Merlin knew that life's lessons are best learned from nature. He also knew that the best way to understand nature was to become one with it. Using his wizard's power, he transformed Arthur into various animals so that the young boy could deeply experience the lessons that each animal has to share.

Guided imagery is a wonderful way to enter into the essence of other forms of life. Experiencing them in our hearts and minds, we find it easier to appreciate their special gifts.

When you create your own guided imagery, remember that the more deeply people become absorbed in the images, the more clearly they'll remember the details. To give your story vividness and clarity, choose words and phrases that refer to the physical senses. When the stories you tell are rich with sights, sounds, tastes, and feelings, the information you weave into the story is sure to be retained for a long time. Allow plenty of time in your narration for the imagination to absorb each scene. Narrating to appropriate background music helps deepen the mood. (For the Tree Imagery I've enjoyed using the following music: Beethoven's *Pastoral Symphony #6*, Vivaldi's *The Four Seasons*, and Pachelbel's *Canon in D*.)

To be truly effective, your imagery should have an expansive quality, so that it lifts the hearer into the realm of inspiring facts and noble thoughts and ideals.

In the imagery that follows, the players imagine themselves to be trees. The narrator describes how the tree's roots and branches reach out from the trunk, deep into the ground and high into the sky. The tree interacts with the forest community of birds, plants, and animals, and through sharing these experiences the "tree" (listener) feels an expansion of awareness that opens his sympathies to other forms of life.

When planning a guided imagery session, ask yourself which quality or lesson you can learn from a particular plant, animal, or natural phenomenon. In your imagery, give special care to bringing out this quality.

Most scientists shy away from "anthropomorphism" and would surely say that trees can't feel and aren't aware of themselves. On the other hand, many poets have attributed human feelings to trees. Much more important than who's right or wrong is what *we* feel when we "become" a tree and do all the things trees do. Our own empathy at least enriches us and helps us cultivate a caring, protective attitude toward the environment.

A tree provides shelter for plants and animals. It even moderates the seasonal temperature extremes, creating a comfortable, inviting habitat for all kinds of creatures. In fact, a single tree nearly always supports and nourishes a whole community of life-forms. "Living" the life of a tree gives us new views of how nature shares unselfishly within the community of life-forms.

Two of the qualities of trees that I admire most are their flexibility and inner strength. Trees can't run away from situations; they must stand firm and face the winter storms. Their roots hold them firmly in place while they patiently endure wind, fire, lightning, and other calamities. In Tree Imagery, people feel what it's like to stand firm and weather adversity, drawing strength from deeply-planted roots. The analogy to human life is instructive, because the players get a feeling for what it's like to reach down inside themselves for inner strength and not let themselves be bowled over by tests and trials.

Tree Imagery

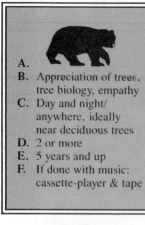

A.
B. Appreciation of trees, tree biology, empathy
C. Day and night/ anywhere, ideally near deciduous trees
D. 2 or more
E. 5 years and up
F. If done with music: cassette-player & tape

TREE IMAGERY CAN BE PLAYED indoors or outdoors. Outdoors, look for a clear area under a deciduous tree—preferably a large one.

Have the players spread out under the tree and stand with their eyes closed, near enough to you that they can easily hear you. Tell them they're about to experience the life of a tree for an entire year—summer, fall, winter and spring. In fact, they're going to *become* a tree.

While you narrate the imagery, the "trees" can hold their arms up like branches, or just stand still with their eyes closed, visualizing. With younger children, movement (for example, during the winter "storms") helps channel restlessness. For further details of Tree Imagery, see the Sample Tree Session, later in the book.

If you can't remember or don't have time to read the complete narration, don't worry. If you memorize a few salient details from each phase of the tree's year-long life cycle, you'll find you can get through occasional memory-lapses by ad-libbing. A book that I've found very helpful as background reading for Tree Imagery is *The Great American Forest*, by Rutherford Platt.

With young children and other groups with short attention spans, shorten your presentation by omitting secondary facts and curtailing some of your mood-setting description. Your skill with Tree Imagery will improve every time you use it.

Tree Imagery Narration: With the group standing under a tree in their chosen positions, begin the guided imagery:

Close your eyes . . .

Trees are very important to life on Earth. They create half the world's oxygen. They hold the soil and prevent erosion. They provide food and shelter for untold billions of animals. They warm their immediate environment in winter and cool it in the summer with their shade. Trees inspire us with thoughts of beauty, nobility, strength, and serenity.

With your eyes closed, in your mind see yourself walking through a forest of large deciduous trees. (Pause) Now you've entered a clearing in the middle of the forest. Stop, turn toward the sun, and feel that you are becoming a large tree in this forest.

Stand with your feet shoulder-distance apart and feel your huge taproot growing down from your hips. Feel it go down through your thighs...your knees...and down through your ankles...down through the soles of your feet and into the earth. Your taproot is working itself through the soft topsoil, and working farther down, down, deep into the clay soil. Keep sinking your taproot farther and farther down into the earth until it's over 30 feet deep. (Pause)

Now, begin sending lateral roots out in all directions, just beneath the surface of the ground. Send them out to the left...to the right...in front...and behind. Spread them out farther and farther —10 feet, 20 feet, past 30 feet from the trunk. (Pause)

Gently sway back and forth. Feel how firmly you're rooted in the earth. (Pause) Mentally look at your large trunk and see how big and round you are. (Pause) Is your bark smooth or rough? Is it dark or light-colored? (Pause)

Now follow your trunk up higher and higher until you come to your biggest branches. Follow them as they divide up into smaller and smaller branches and spread out into the sky.

It's summertime, and life is easy. The days are long. The sun is warm. A light breeze blows your branches gently back and forth. Feel how your roots hold you firmly anchored to the earth.

What kind of leaves do you have? Are they large and pointed? Or are they small and round?

Absorb energy from the sun's warm rays. Bring it into your leaves and make food, using sunlight, air, and water that you've brought up from the ground. Now send the food you've made in your leaves down through your branches to your trunk. Feel it going down and down, all the way to your roots. Store it there. Summer is the time when you store food. (You stopped growing many months ago, before the end of spring.)

Deep in the earth, gather water from the soil using your tiny root hairs. Your root hairs spread out and touch nearly every particle of soil around you. Bring this moisture up. Feel it rise first in tiny streams, then as vast rivers of moisture. Now it's surging up the trunk, racing higher and higher up the trunk at speeds of up to a hundred miles per hour, and out through the branches and into the leaves. Now it evaporates from your leaves, permeating the atmosphere all around you with moisture. As autumn approaches, the days grow short and the sunlight is less intense. Food production finally comes to a complete halt. It's getting cooler, and the sap in your leaves is starting to descend, down out of your branches and into your trunk, and to your roots below. There, deep in your roots, the sap is stored for next spring.

Watch as your abandoned leaves turn golden, yellow, or red. What is happening is not new—you've dropped your leaves in autumn many times through the years. Cast off your leaves and become dormant now. You are preparing yourself, protecting yourself from the approaching cold of winter. (Pause)

Storm clouds come rolling over the horizon, darkening the sky. The wind begins to push at your upper branches. The rain patters in big drops and then pounds at your naked branches with their few remaining leaves. A fierce wind rips through the forest and tears off many leaves, driving them to the ground. Look down at the forest floor. It's covered with your brightly-colored leaves and leaves from the trees around you. (Pause) The storm breaks, and your branches are completely soaked. Hear the water drip from limb to limb on its way to the ground. (Pause)

Winter isn't over yet. An even bigger storm blows in from the sea. Listen to the roar of its approach. Powerful gusts rattle your branches and toss them about. Like a ship on an angry sea, you rock back and forth, back and forth, back and forth. Only your big taproot and large lateral roots keep you from crashing to the ground.

The storm is beginning to blow itself out. The wind is slackening. Once more, the forest is quiet. Your branches are almost bare now, and the ground is painted gold, yellow, and red. Your stark silhouette stands out against the somber gray winter sky. One by one, your last leaves fall off and gently roll and tumble to the earth. The temperature drops, and snow begins to fall. Feel the snow as it piles up on your branches.

All animal life has left the forest. Many of the insects have died. Most of the birds have flown south. The mammals are either hibernating or have gone down to the warmer valleys. You, too, have died back to only 1% of your living tissue—to a thin thread of life just inside your bark. (Pause)

But already stored in your tiny buds are next year's leaves and flowers. See them on the tips of your branches, protected from the cold and wet of winter by a waxy sheath. These buds are your new life for the coming year. Crouch down. Kneel down and become a tiny leaf bud. You're like a baby in its mother's womb, waiting for your time, waiting for spring. (Pause)

The days are becoming longer and warmer. When the temperature and sunlight are just right, the sap deep in the tree's roots awakens and surges up through the trunk, racing higher and higher, emerging into the branches and entering the buds. (Pause) Unfold now as a tiny, tender, bright-green spring leaflet. Open up completely to the spring sun and receive its warming, energy-giving rays. Feel the sun's energy and nourishment, and grow green, grow large.

Send food energy down to the rest of the tree. Now, feel all the leaves in one branch and give to the tree the vitality you feel from the sun.

Become the whole tree again. Feel your roots as they reach deeper into the earth. (Pause) Feel the tips of your branches growing. You are growing from both ends—and a little around the middle! Spring is the time of renewal. Now 99% of your body has come back to life, adding tremendous vitality to yourself and to the forest.

With your renewal, animals and plants return to the forest. Birds land in your branches. Reach out with one of your branches and let a robin land on you. Deer are feeding around your trunk. Wildflowers are pushing up and out from the earth beneath you. All animal life depends on you for food, shelter—and, yes, even a sense of well-being. Spread your branches out to all living things in the forest, in a spirit of protection and love. Feel that you share one life together, in beauty and harmony. (Pause)

Please lie down on your back. I'm going to read a poem about trees. Feel that you're becoming the part of the tree that each line describes. After the first stanza, you can open your eyes and look at the base of a large tree.

Roots going down,
reaching
through damp earth deep.
Down, down,
holding me here.

Open your eyes
and look at the trunk
of a large tree . . .

My great round trunk,
massive and slender,
solid yet yielding,
carrier of life.

My long limbs
stretching out for space,
tips tickled by the wind,
touched by the sun.

They invite all life
to shelter among them,
beneath them, inside me,
beneath me.

Life runs through me.
I invite all life to me.

Roots anchored deep.
limbs lofty high,
I abide in both worlds
of earth and sky.

A.
B. Aesthetic appreciation, trust, seeing clearly
C. Day/outdoor area
D. 2 or more
E. 3 years and up
F. Index cards and pencils

Camera

CAMERA IS ONE OF THE MOST POWERFUL and enjoyable activities in this book. In a simple and natural way, it quiets distracting thoughts and restlessness and frees the attention for absorbing nature with unobstructed clarity.

One player takes the role of photographer, and the other plays the camera. The photographer guides the camera, who keeps his eyes closed, on a search for beautiful and interesting pictures. When the photographer sees something he likes, he points the camera's lens (eyes) at it, framing the object he wants to "shoot." Then he presses the shutter button (see below) to open the lens.

It's important that the camera keep his eyes closed between pictures, so that the 3- to 5-second "exposure" will have the impact of surprise. Many people have told me they remembered their "pictures" fondly for years after playing the game.

Encourage the photographers to be creative in choosing and framing pictures. Tell them, "You can make stunning photographs by taking shots from unusual angles and perspectives. For example, you can both lie down under a tree and take your picture looking upward, or you can put your camera very close to a tree's bark or leaves. Try looking down into a flower, or panning the horizon. Be open to the opportunities of the moment."

Sometimes while playing the Camera Game and playing the photographer's role, I've used a bird call (see "Bird Calling" in *Sharing Nature with Children*) to attract birds to within a few feet, then take their pictures with my "camera."

Because the Camera Game uses nature experiences instead of verbal explanations, very young children can participate just as fully as adults. It's very touching to watch five-year-olds guide their parents or grandparents, taking pictures and sharing their delight in natural things.

I suggest that children "press the shutter button" by tapping the camera's shoulder. A second tap tells the camera to close his eyes. For the first picture, it may help to say "Open" with the first tap, and "Close" with the second.

In a mixed group of adults and children, or children of varied ages, I ask the players to use the tragus (the flap of cartilage at the front of the ear) as the shutter button. I don't generally recommend the tragus with small children because of the temptation to stick fingers in one another's ears!

The preferred "exposure time" is 3 to 5 seconds. With longer exposures, the camera's mind begins to wander, reducing the impact of the picture—just as too much light overexposes real film.

Show the players how to pan the camera—i.e., move it slowly with the shutter held open, like a movie camera. While panning, they may keep the shutter open longer than five seconds, since the movement will hold the camera's interest. Suggest that they also pan vertically —for example, starting at the base of a tree and slowly moving up the trunk to the highest branches, then into the sky.

The photographers can prepare their cameras for the next picture by telling them which lens to use. For a picture of a flower, tell the camera to choose a close-up lens; for a sweeping scenic panorama, a wide-angle lens; and for a far-away object, a telephoto lens.

Take time to talk to the group about the elements of creative and beautiful pictures—otherwise they may end up with pictures of deer scat or the insides of trash cans! This is especially important with small children. It's also very important to encourage the photographers and cameras to talk only when it's unavoidable. Explain that silence creates pictures that have greater impact for the camera.

You may need to take time to show the group how to guide their "blind" cameras sensitively and protectively. I've found it works well to hold the camera's hand and gently pull an arm in the direction you want to go.

Tell the photographers they'll have about 10 minutes to take pictures, then they'll trade roles. It works well to tell the photographers to take a certain number of pictures (six to ten is fine), then trade places with their partners. With these rules, everyone will finish at about the same time.

After everyone has played both roles, give each player a 3×5 index card and tell them, "Remember one of the pictures you took when you played camera. Develop it by drawing it, and give it to the photographer." If some players groan self-consciously about their lack of artistic talent, tell them they can blame the quality of their pictures on the photographer!

The goal of the game is to give the players a more lively appreciation of nature's beauty. You can extend the game by asking the group to write about their pictures. You might also have the photographers take 8–10 pictures on a single theme: plant succession, animal homes, or conifers, for instance. The camera can then write a story in which he must use all the pictures. Afterwards, the camera and photographer can discuss their stories.

You can have all the players be cameras at the same time. Have them hold onto a rope and pull them along gently to the next picture with their eyes closed. Ask everyone to turn in the direction of the subject ("Please turn left"), then take a picture with one camera at a time. (Make sure the people at the end of the rope don't sway off the trail when you turn.) The number of players you can guide will depend on the age of the group and the terrain.

Living History

CHIEF SEATTLE

RACHEL CARSON

GEORGE WASHINGTON CARVER

John Muir
Earth-plane
Universe

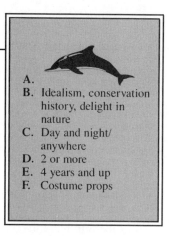

EVERYONE, but children especially, is greatly influenced by role models. Uplifting stories from people's lives, shared with heart and spirit, awaken and expand our vision of what is possible and true. The life stories of the great naturalists are a wonderful tool for bringing alive not only inspiring nature wisdom and experiences, but a sense of the value of living by high ideals.

A.
B. Idealism, conservation history, delight in nature
C. Day and night/ anywhere
D. 2 or more
E. 4 years and up
F. Costume props

In my own work, I've developed full-length storytelling sessions about John Muir, George Washington Carver, and Saint Francis of Assisi. It's been very rewarding to see how deeply touched people are by Carver's almost mystical attunement with and love for the plant world, his selfless service to humanity, and his unconquerable spirit; by St. Francis's brotherly love and respect for all manifestations of the Creator, including birds, trees, and wind, and his compassion that led him more than once to trade his only cloak for a suffering animal's comfort and safety, or to give away his frugal meal for their sustenance; and by John Muir's tremendous joy and delight in nature, along with his profound experiences and many wilderness adventures.

You, too, can share these wonderful lives and those of your own heroes in the environmental movement, by simply studying their biographies and telling their stories in your own words.

Simple props create the atmosphere of another era. I've memorized long passages from the writings of the characters I play, to give the audience a direct experience of what that person was really like. I even put on clothing that suggests the character I'm portraying. I've also found it very effective to introduce an imaginary second character, a friend of the hero, who tells anecdotes about the hero's life that he himself would probably be too modest to share. My Muir program is called *John Muir and a Friend*, for example.

Choose characters whose life stories give you real joy. That way, you'll be able to pour sincere, unforced enthusiasm into your presentation. Select some quotations, experiences in nature, and a variety of funny and interesting stories from your character's life. You can make your first presentations very short, perhaps including them as a

---

Nature Activities

minor part of some other presentation. Gradually, as you gain confidence, you can expand your "show."

Memorize some passages from your character's own spoken and written words. You can begin with a few resounding one-liners. Learn the plots of a few stories from the hero's life that reinforce the main points of your presentation. But don't try to memorize all your lines. That's usually a mistake, since you'll probably be rigid with tension if you feel you have to recall the exact words of a script. Instead, remember the main points, then just spontaneously follow the inspiration you feel from the story. Just learn the story well enough that you can relax and have fun while you tell it.

As the words of the memorized quotations become familiar, you'll find you can put increasing depth of feeling into them and make them come more and more alive for your listeners. It's easy to memorize by repeating the words slowly with your eyes closed, *feeling* and *visualizing* their meaning.

Actors use a technique called "emotional recall" to improve their performances. You might like to try it. Remember a personal experience that evokes a feeling appropriate to the story you're trying to memorize. Recall your exact feelings at the time, then say the words of your presentation with this same feeling. For example, in my John Muir program, I tell how Muir saw the Great Central Valley of California for the first time. It was spring. The valley was an endless sea of flowers, and Muir's description is one of the most thrilling in his journals. If you were narrating this scene, you could practice by remembering your own feelings when you first looked at some similar scene. Here are Muir's words:

"*. . .one shining morning, a landscape was displayed that after all my wanderings still appears as the most beautiful I have ever beheld. At my feet lay the Great Central Valley of California. . . level and flowery, like a lake of pure sunshine, 40 and 50 miles wide, 500 miles long. And from the eastern boundary of this vast golden flower-bed rose the mighty Sierra, miles in height and so gloriously colored and so radiant, it seemed not clothed with light, but wholly composed of it, like the wall of some celestial city.*"

MORE TECHNIQUES FOR GOOD STORYTELLING

- Memorize the beginning and ending. This will help you start confidently and finish strongly. Space your best stories throughout

the presentation to sustain the listeners' interest.
- Plan your stage entry.
- Show and tell. Spend less time on verbal description.
- Deeply feel the special mood or quality of a story before telling it. Give each story a single, focused point. Tell a variety of stories with different points.
- Discover the "profound moment" of each story, and time its

presentation carefully to allow the audience to savor that moment fully
- Don't try to tell everything about your subject. Simplify your stories. Omit stories that don't really add to the central message of your presentation. Give the most power and the fullest treatment to the ones that have real impact.
- Keep positive eye-contact. Exceptions: You're portraying dialogue between characters, or you're acting a scene and drawing the audience into the action.
- Change your voice and character by changing your consciousness. The audience will believe you to the degree that you yourself believe and become what you're acting.
- Use your eyes and face to express a character's qualities.
- Use your hands to create space and dimension, or to paint pictures. Expand your role with gestures, embellishing and punctuating your points. Make gestures large and away from the body, so people sitting in the back rows can see.
- Change your speech, rhythm, and mood frequently. By varying the pace, you'll keep your "act" interesting. Slow down a bit from time to time to give the audience a chance to rest.
- Pause for emphasis and suspense. Calm control will enable you to give each word the full power of expression.
- Don't panic if you forget your lines. Just pause, think, and keep eye-contact. The more relaxed you are, the better you'll be able to recover gracefully.
- Use humor—it relaxes an audience and makes them open and receptive to your message. The best time to make meaningful, serious points is often just after telling a funny story.
- Adapt your show for different age-groups. Children think in physical and visual terms; adults are more interested in verbal meanings. Children take longer to recover from funny stories.
- Share *with* your audience, rather than performing *to* them. Focus on sharing with them the delight and joy that you feel in your story.

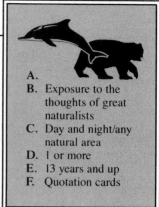

A.
B. Exposure to the thoughts of great naturalists
C. Day and night/any natural area
D. 1 or more
E. 13 years and up
F. Quotation cards

Nature Meditations

WE WERE DEEP in the woods of Great Smoky Mountain National Park, on a tiny island with water rushing by on one side and a serene pond on the other—a magical place, perfect for Nature Meditations. The fifty people in our group were absorbed in the surrounding beauty. Some were sitting on rocks in the stream; others were under the trees, gazing across the pond. Everyone seemed calm and wholly attentive. Each of us had selected a card on which was printed an inspiring thought and a nature meditation that we could use to focus our awareness. Later, we shared our experiences and insights. Even with a group as large as ours was, there was a remarkable mood of silent communion with nature. It was heartwarming to see such a sincere desire to draw inspiration from the natural world. Nature Meditations is one of my favorite activities for creating this kind of contemplative atmosphere.

To play Nature Meditations, you'll need to collect a number of inspiring sayings and write them on index cards, one saying per card. Each saying should have an accompanying activity that helps the reader translate the idea into personal experience. Avoid sayings that are too abstract and mental. If you don't have enough different quotations to give each person a unique one, it's okay to give your most effective ones to more than one person. You might want to draw from *Listening to Nature*, which offers nearly 30 quotations with

---

Nature Activities

suggested activities. These sayings and their accompanying meditations are from that book:

"My heart is tuned to the quietness that the stillness of nature inspires."–H. I. Khan. Find a quiet place, where you can be alone. Listen to the sounds around you. *Listen also for the silences between sounds.* When your mind wanders, repeat the above saying. It will help to bring you back to the present moment.

"Holy Earth Mother, the trees and all nature are witnesses of your thoughts and deeds."—Winnebago Indians. John Muir said, "Every natural object is a conductor of divinity." Go for a walk, silently repeating this Winnebago prayer of reverence for the earth and its Creator. When an animal, plant, rock, or beautiful scene draws your attention, stop, and silently offer thanks for the joy and beauty you feel.

Find a quiet place where each player can be alone. A beautiful site helps the players tune in to the inspiration of their quotation.

When you're ready to play, turn the cards face down and let each player choose a card. Tell them to feel that the quotation they've drawn is meant especially for them. If they can't relate to the thought expressed on the card, it's all right to let them choose another. But it's surprising how often people choose quotations that seem just right.

The players usually understand that Nature Meditations is a quiet activity, but you may need to give a gentle reminder of this.

I generally allow 10–15 minutes for reflection, then I call the group back together and ask them to sit in a circle and tell what they've experienced.

I also find it works well to use a printed card that has several quotations and meditations and let the players choose their own. I used 12 quotations and activities from **Listening to Nature** to design such a card, which is available from the publishers, along with a set of cards with single quotations.

"*The best and most beautiful things in the world cannot be seen or even touched. They must be felt with the heart.*"—HELEN KELLER

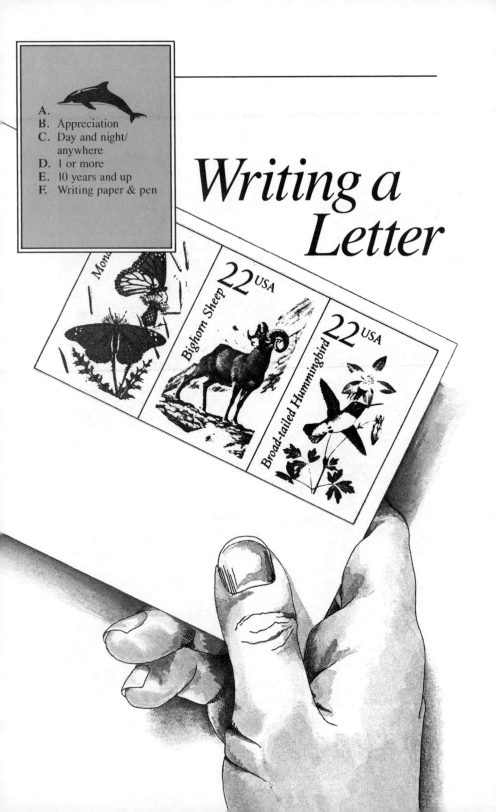

A.
B. Appreciation
C. Day and night/ anywhere
D. 1 or more
E. 10 years and up
F. Writing paper & pen

Writing a Letter

WRITING A LETTER is a great way to end a nature experience that lasts several days. (It's for players 13 years and older.)

To begin, you can explain the activity like this:

"We've shared deep experiences of nature. You've probably had insights and experiences that made you feel, 'I never want to forget this!'

"We're going back to our active, demanding lives. The immediacy of these nature experiences will fade. Let's write letters to ourselves, telling everything we might want to remember a few weeks from now. Your letter will be completely confidential. We'll mail it to you in two weeks."

This activity has two worthwhile effects: Writing the letter impresses the experience and its lessons on the players' minds, and receiving the letter reinforces their enthusiasm for continuing their contact with the natural world.

This is from a letter written by a member of a nature pilgrimage my wife and I led through the slickrock country of the American Southwest:

To myself,

"I have had a wonderful time these past ten days enjoying and experiencing nature. The people are all so easy and friendly to be with.

"My best and most moving experience was hiking the Lower Calf Creek Falls Trail. While walking alone with no other member of the group in sight, I looked up at the enormous walls of the canyon and truly felt a divine presence. The strength, grandeur, and timelessness of the walls of the canyon was quite profound for me. I felt guided into the waterfall by these great walls. . . .

"I want to keep the memories of this trip with me—to give me calmness, so I can feel nature in my everyday activities and not lose the feelings of closeness."

Yours truly,
Diane

The Birds
of the Air

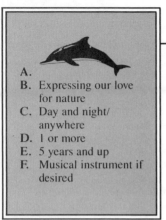

A.
B. Expressing our love for nature
C. Day and night/ anywhere
D. 1 or more
E. 5 years and up
F. Musical instrument if desired

CELEBRATING with songs and poems makes a fitting close for a nature outing. After the reflective stage, the players feel the uplifted thoughts and moods that nature inspires. By celebrating these feelings, the players become more deeply aware of them. Spend some time quietly absorbing the meaning of the songs and poems you've chosen. This will help you to communicate their inspiration.

Feel free to share your own poetry and music. Many folk songs have inspiring nature themes. And you'll find many inspiring poems and sayings in *Listening to Nature*.

I'd like to share a poem I wrote, called *The Birds of the Air*. I wrote it to help me remember the harmony of the nature world and feel that harmony inside. When I'm out in nature, I frequently spend a long time repeating this poem over and over silently, while I walk or sit watching some beautiful scene. Groups of children and adults seem to enjoy it, too.

THE BIRDS OF THE AIR

The birds of the air
  are my brothers,
All flowers my sisters,
The trees are my friends.

All living creatures,
Mountains and streams,
I take unto my care.

For this green earth is our mother,
Hidden in the sky is the spirit above.

I share one Life with all who are here;
To everyone I give my love,
To everyone I give my love.

THE BIRDS OF THE AIR
words *by* Joseph Cornell
music *by* Michael Starner-Simpson

The birds of the air are my bro - thers, All flow-ers my sis-ters, the

trees are my friends. All liv-ing crea-tures, mountains and streams,

I take un-to my care. For this green earth is our mo-ther,

hid-den in the sky is the spi-rit a-bove.

I share one life wi- ith all who are here; to ev-ry-one I give my

love, to ev-ry-one I give my love.

If you'd like to use this poem for personal reflection, try repeating or singing it silently or aloud as you walk or sit in nature. Feel the meaning of the words. Project your feelings out to your surroundings. As you do so, you'll find a deep brotherly love coming into your heart and flowing out to the birds, trees, and flowers.

When you recite *The Birds of the Air* or other poems to a group, find a quiet place where natural beauty draws out the group's higher feelings. Form a circle or line with the participants facing outward, each looking in a direction that pleases him. You can sing with the group, or invite them to repeat the words responsively, one phrase at a time. (If you want to do both, I recommend reciting the poem alone first, then singing it together.) Encourage everyone to project out to his surroundings thoughts of friendship and love.

Whether you're a nature educator or a nature enthusiast, the most effective thing you can do for the Earth is cultivate love for all living things. Love fires our enthusiasm to take nature into our care. It fills us with a vibrant, living power that communicates Nature's joy and wonder as no mere words ever can.

Wyatt, my friend who takes care of a fruit orchard, told me he was changing the irrigation pipes one day, when two little birds flew right up to him and began fluttering around his head. At first this made him only vaguely curious, but as he went on working the birds became increasingly insistent. Wyatt realized the birds wanted to show him something, so he let himself be led to the far side of the orchard, a hundred yards away.

Arriving at one of the trees, the birds immediately flew high up in the branches. Wyatt was following as fast as he could. He climbed up after them and discovered a large gopher snake that had just finished raiding the birds' nest.

Wyatt said he was sorry he hadn't understood the birds sooner so that he could have saved their young. He was deeply touched that they had come and asked for his help. He told me he thought the birds must have seen him working in the orchard every day, and had probably come to think of him as the orchard's protector.

Nature responds to us when we approach her with love and respect. I was sitting with a small group of friends looking out across a small lake in the high Sierra recently. It was a rainy November afternoon, and the mist had kept us from seeing the distant shore. Finally, the sun broke through the clouds and seemed to bring the lake to life. Fish began jumping in the sparkling water. Several flocks of birds flew by, right in front of us. Red shrubs and yellow willows ringed the lake, adding their vibrant colors to the green and gray of the conifers and rock cliffs. The lake and its surroundings radiated vitality and life, a striking contrast to the drab storm sky we'd seen all day. After ten minutes the mists returned, again shrouding our view.

We had been doing contemplative activities from *Listening to Nature*. This was the only time we'd seen the sun all day, and because it happened just when we were feeling most attentive and appreciative, we felt that nature had lovingly responded with this beautiful moment.

Not long ago, I heard about a musician who invited a group of people to go for a walk in the forest. When they returned, he asked his companions if they had heard the birds singing. They hadn't, so he took them out again, this time urging them to listen attentively for bird song. This time, they heard the birds. They said, "Perhaps we simply weren't paying attention the first time." But the musician had recorded the sounds of the forest both times. When he played back the recording of the first walk, everyone was amazed to learn that there truly hadn't been any birds singing. The musician explained that the birds hadn't sung because no one had been listening for them, and that it was their appreciation during the second walk that had caused them to sing so beautifully.

I've been amazed, after using The Birds of the Air, how often large numbers of birds have flown into the nearby trees and began singing all around us. It has happened too many times to believe that it's merely coincidence.

Activities like The Birds of the Air—in which people can, by expressing their loving and appreciative thoughts, discover a living, reciprocal relationship with the natural world—are extremely valuable, for the people themselves, and also, I believe, for the continued well-being of the Earth itself.

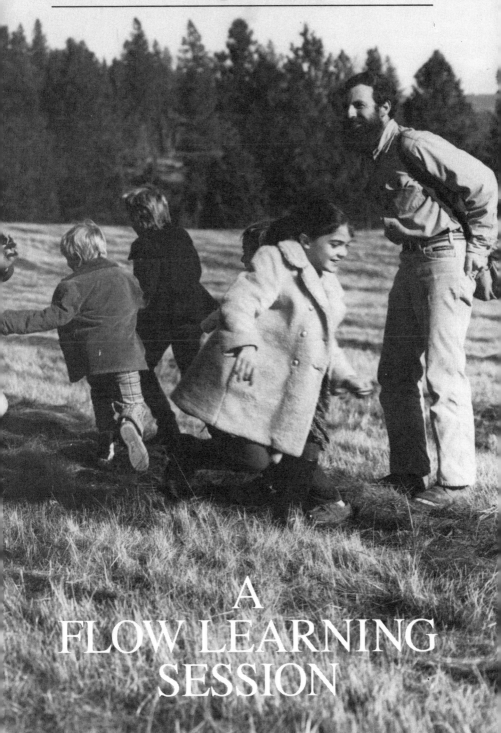

Chapter IV

A
FLOW LEARNING
SESSION

I T'S IMPORTANT TO PROVIDE a sense of continuity between the Flow Learning activities. Weaving the activities together in a purposeful, carefully-designed sequence gives people a much richer, more satisfying experience of Flow Learning. In a well-designed session, each activity builds toward a truly uplifting, memorable experience of nature. By contrast, if you use the activities without any thought to their appropriate selection and order, you'll find your outings much less satisfying and enjoyable.

When your primary goal is to encourage a sense of wonder, factual learning takes a secondary, supportive role. But with a bit of creative planning, you can make your sessions both uplifting and educational. In fact, a combination of the two is usually the most satisfying for both the leader and the participants.

The following series of forest activities gives people both scientific and intuitive appreciation of trees. My purpose in sharing them is to show you how certain activities follow and complement one another, providing a far richer and more dynamic learning experience than a selection chosen haphazardly.

TREES

As I've said many times, the activities you choose should be matched with the group's age and size, and the surrounding environment. With just a few people, you can sometimes safely begin with forest experiences, but in a large group it may be necessary first to play some games to create enthusiastic participation.

With children, it's especially important to begin with a lively, fun activity. If the children already have learned something about trees, a game they'll enjoy is Owls and Crows. It's exciting, and it stimulates children's curiosity about trees.

To play, divide the group into two teams. Have the teams stand on opposite sides of a rope laid out straight on the ground. One team is the Owls and the other is the Crows. You'll say a statement aloud, and if it's true the Owls chase the Crows. If it's false, the Crows chase the Owls. Anyone who's tagged before he gets past the home base line (about 10–15 feet behind the rope) has to go over to the other side. (Complete instructions for Owls and Crows are given in *Sharing Nature with Children*.)

The statements should be simple and clearly true or false. Some examples:
1. "Pines lose their leaves in summer."
2. "Acorns come from oak trees."
3. "Cottonwoods grow best in dry, rocky places."
4. "Firs, hemlocks and pines are all evergreen trees."
5. "The leaf I have in my hand is from a buckeye tree."

The children learn new facts and concepts, while having a delightful and energizing time.

For older children and adults, the Animal Clue Game (see page 52) is another excellent way to ensure participation, because the clues create lots of interest in trees. Some examples:
1. "I am very old, and I'm the tallest living thing."
2. "I set the pace for other trees: I'm among the first to get my leaves in the spring and to lose them in the fall."
3. "My seeds are about the size of golf balls."
4. "A broken branch of mine can take root along a river bank and grow into a tree."

(Answers: 1. Redwood, 2. and 3. Buckeye; 4. Willow.)

Two games for introducing people to trees are Meet a Tree and Blind Trail. These games give the players a wonderful direct experience of trees that creates a high level of enthusiasm for other tree activities.

Meet a Tree: In Meet a Tree, you blindfold your partner and walk him to a tree, let him feel it, then return to where you started. Take off his blindfold and have him find *his* tree. (For a complete description, see *Sharing Nature with Children*.)

Relying on faculties other than sight to get to know a tree makes a profound impact on the players. Children at a camp where I used to work would return year after year and lead me deep into the forest with great enthusiasm to show me "their" tree.

Blind Trail: The Blind Trail Game gives people plenty of time to meet a tree. It's especially powerful because it induces a calm, receptive mood. The players walk quietly through the forest by

themselves, blindfolded and guided only by a rope. The trail should wind around interestingly and take the player to a variety of rocks, bushes, and trees.

To play Blind Trail, you'll need a safe, open area or a trail, ideally with a variety of large trees. (See *Sharing Nature with Children* for complete instructions.)

Build a Tree: Build a Tree is another excellent way to teach the

different parts of a tree. It gives the players a greater appreciation of how trees function. It's also a perfect lead-in for Tree Imagery, because it creates wonderful group spirit and helps people feel less self-conscious during the Tree Imagery visualization. Build a Tree and Tree Imagery complement each other wonderfully, because in Build a Tree the players learn scientific facts and principles, and in Tree Imagery they acquire information through direct experiences of feeling and intuition.

After Tree Imagery, when the players have finished sharing what it was like to be a tree, you can build on the receptive mood with an inspirational activity. Here are some suggestions:

- Sing or lead a group repetition of The Birds of the Air.
- Play the Nature Meditations Game, using tree quotations.
- Tell stories.

A wonderful tree story is *The Man Who Planted Hope and Grew Happiness*. Or perhaps you might like to talk about John Muir's love for trees. Muir knew his trees so well that he could identify many species by listening to the distinctive "wind music" the breeze made as it moved through their branches.

After playing these games, you'll find the group much more attentive during a nature walk to identify and share technical information about trees.

In the series of tree games presented above, Stage 1 (Awaken Enthusiasm) is represented by Owls and Crows and the Animal Clue Game. If you think it would be a good idea to calm the group down before doing sensitive and experiential activities, try leading the group in Sound Map, which is an excellent Stage 2 (Focus Attention) activity.

Meet a Tree, Blind Trail, and Tree Imagery are Stage 3 (Direct Experience) activities. Build a Tree is really an Enthusiasm game, but I saved it for later in this series of tree activities because it's such a perfect introduction to Tree Imagery. Birds of the Air, Nature Meditations, and story-telling are all examples of Stage 4 (Share Inspiration).

I've found that nearly all adults and most children can appreciate these sensitive activities. With younger children, though, you'll probably want to shorten Tree Imagery and replace the Quotation activity with something else. With a *lively* group of children, you may want to forego activities like Tree Imagery altogether, and instead emphasize more active games. The chart below gives other activities from *Sharing Nature with Children* that you might like to use during a forest outing.

GAMES FOR FOREST HIKES

(These games are described in *Sharing Nature with Children*.)

Awaken Enthusiasm: Duplication, Identification Game
Focus Attention: Unnature Trail, Sounds
Direct Experience: Caterpillar Walk, Blind Walk
Share Inspiration: Recipe for a Forest

A SAMPLE FLOW LEARNING SESSION

If you'd like to try teaching a Flow Learning session, you might find it helpful to start with the sample sequence that follows. (To put together your own sequences, see the Flow Learning Activity chart in the Appendix, which lists all the activities from *Sharing Nature with Children, Sharing Nature with Children II,* and *Listening to Nature.*

The Animal Clue Game requires reading, so you might want to skip it for young children. Adults and children alike will enjoy the rest of the activities:

Awaken Enthusiasm: Animal Clue Game, Animals, Animals!
Focus Attention: Build a Tree, Sound Map
Direct Experience: Camera, Mystery Animal
Share Inspiration: The Birds of the Air

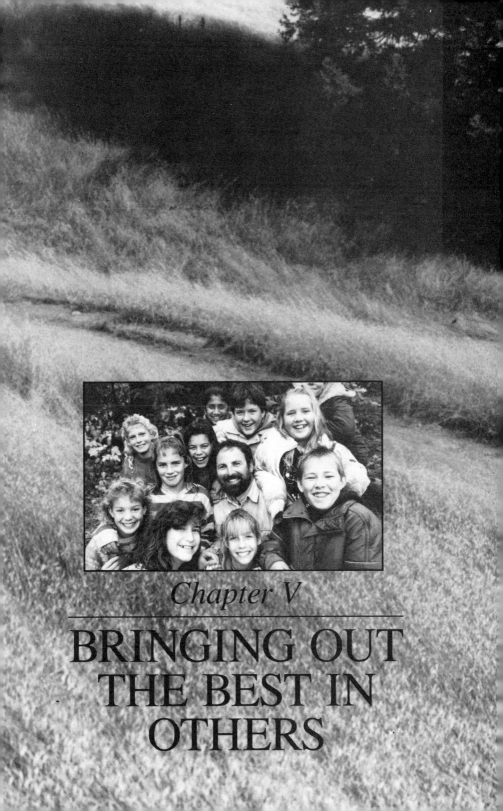

Chapter V

BRINGING OUT THE BEST IN OTHERS

*"If you treat an individual as he is, he will stay that way,
but if you treat him as if he were what he could be,
he will become what he could be."*
—GOETHE

S O FAR, I haven't mentioned two key ingredients in every effective nature activity and Flow Learning experience. If I were to omit them, I'd feel I had neglected to share the central principles of working with people in nature.

The first is the *attitude* with which we teach. As I said earlier, the word "education" comes from the Greek for "to draw out." To draw out people's enthusiasm for nature activities, we need to approach them with a feeling of deep inspiration. We ourselves must feel the love and concern for nature that we hope to awaken in others.

The second principle is to see in everyone the potential for deep appreciation for nature while accepting him where he is, then helping him take the next step toward greater awareness.

Given the seriousness of today's environmental problems, it's natural to want to influence others to accept certain specific ecological points of view. But as teachers, it's important to be aware that we can only ever be really effective by approaching our students on the level of their own realities and convincing them of the relevance of our teaching goals. By first understanding them, we can more clearly know what *they* need in order to achieve greater understanding.

At a camp in the High Sierras, where I was a naturalist, we once hosted a group of boys from a very tough, inner-city neighborhood. They were a fairly hostile bunch, accustomed to swearing at each other, and "enjoying" their days at camp by using their knives on tent ropes, trees, and frogs in the nearby creek. (Their idea of a nature hike was more on the lines of a nature *hunt*.)

When the time came for our scheduled nature outing, I wasn't looking forward with much enthusiasm to the event. They evidently weren't, either, because they didn't show up. I finally found them in the camp meadow, hunting wildlife along the creek. As I approached, I let go of all my preconceptions about a typical nature hike. Instead, I tried to tune in to the boys' energy.

Because they were so excitable, I felt it would be best to start with something active and involving. I wanted to turn their energy, which was focused on aggressive, destructive activities, toward wholesome adventures and challenges.

Before my arrival, they'd been having a good time on their own, so I decided to show them right off that our time together could be fun, too. I took them to an area of the creek where the banks were several feet high and introduced them to one of the camp's favorite sports: broad jumping from one bank to the other. If you failed to make the other shore, a mud bath was your reward.

Luckily, everyone succeeded in crossing the creek. There were some exciting moments when the smaller boys almost didn't make the jump, but standing safely on the other bank, we all laughed happily. In a subtle way, our satisfaction over our individual success drew us closer together.

The ridge above the camp was a good place to look for deer, pine martens, marmots, hawks, and golden eagles. I told the boys that we'd have to climb a steep cliff to get there. I knew the boys wouldn't refuse the challenge. They eagerly agreed, and we set off to climb the cliff.

The cliff wasn't dangerous, but it posed a challenge for city boys who'd never been in the mountains. The climb required teamwork and a lot of consideration for your climbing-mates. This was the first time I'd seen the boys really work together. The concentration and physical exercise required by the climb helped calm their energies, and when we gathered at the top, they were in a much better mood to observe wildlife.

We didn't see any golden eagles, but we did see one marmot, three deer, and a hawk. We had a spectacular view of a wonderland of lakes, granite domes, forests, and glaciated valleys. For the first time, the boys were genuinely touched by the beauty of their surroundings, and they began eagerly exploring the area. They made so many discoveries that I could barely respond to all their excited calls for information. Then, at the top of the ridge we made a discovery that amazed the boys more than anything else they'd seen.

As we ascended the ridge, the boys were astonished by the dwarfed and twisted trees that seemed barely able to survive on the desolate, windswept rocks. I explained that the winter winds were fierce here, and that the trees took the full blast of the storms. I told them some of the ways trees adapt to wind and cold. Their branches were flexible, so snow and wind couldn't break them. The trees stayed small, hugging the ground to escape the high winds.

To let the boys experience this, we gently bent the branches of a silver pine into a loop. Then we lay down on the rock to feel how much warmer and more protected the ground was than the air above. We pushed the branches of a fully grown, three-foot-tall huckleberry oak to the ground to see why heavy snowfall can't break its branches. The boys were amazed that many of the trees were only a little taller than they were, though perhaps 50 times as old.

The boys were fascinated by the trees' silhouettes, which looked like flags, with most of the branches growing on the leeward side, away from the prevailing winds. We stood in the wind and imagined what it was like for a tree to withstand the violent winter storms, with the wind-hurled ice crystals scouring its branches.

They began to appreciate and empathize deeply with the trees, marveling at their ability to adapt to extreme conditions on the mountain. The trees came alive for them, as unique beings, each with an impressive story to tell. Now the boys, instead of being thoughtless and unfeeling, had come to respect and love the forest.

The boys' dramatic turnaround in behavior taught me how crucial it is to *believe in everyone's potential for goodness.* The more we believe in people's high potential, the more effectively we can draw out their highest feelings and aspirations.

I could have given up on the boys during the first five minutes of our hike. But I knew that nature has a wonderful ability to uplift people. John Muir expressed it well, when he said, "Few are altogether blind and deaf to the sweet looks and voices of nature. There is love of wild Nature in everybody. . ."

Bringing out the best in others also means being completely, sensitively focused on their needs. To be able to do this, we have to free ourselves of personal preferences for doing things in particular ways.

I once visited a rest home for the elderly in Yuba City, California, where I gave a slide presentation of the waterfowl refuges nearby. After the first few slides, I realized from their comments that most of them had grown up in the area. In fact, they had so many stories of what the Sacramento Valley was like in their youth that I stopped my presentation altogether and just listened to their reminiscences. One gentleman told me his parents remembered that in wet winters the valley was one vast lake from the Coast Range all the way to the Sierra Nevada foothills. A person could row a boat from one mountain range to the other. All of them remembered hearing the thrilling clamor of hundreds of thousands of geese and ducks flying over their homes and descending into the marshes. At times, they said, it had looked as if the whole sky were moving.

I grew up in the same valley at a time when there were very few remaining wild places. The waterfowl populations, though still dramatic, were only a fraction of what they had once been. So I was extremely pleased to hear their first-hand accounts of what the valley was like when it was wild.

As the local men and women told their stories, I was struck by how alive and animated they became. The opportunity to share their unique knowledge of the valley was rewarding for them. By resisting the temptation to plow ahead with my planned program, resenting their many comments as interruptions, I had the joy of seeing the group respond to the subject I'd come to talk about much more enthusiastically than if I had continued to speak. I was also able to learn something new.

As a teacher, I've discovered that when I'm sensitive to other people's realities, I can tailor the learning situation and respond specifically to their needs. This makes teaching more creative, stimulating, and joyful. We connect with people much more powerfully when we help them touch something deep inside themselves. In this kind of learning, there's never the frustration and drain associated with trying to "teach" people whether they're interested in the subject or not. This magic happens when we ask ourselves, "How can I reach *this* person? What will help *these* people the most? What is the next step *for them*?" Everyone is interested in something. Your role is like that of a detective who's trying to find out what will especially interest and motivate a particular group.

Another thing that can help us bring out the best in others is trying to accept them totally, regardless of their faults. When we avoid criticizing people (even mentally) for how they are or for the things they do, we remain open to them, and they sense this clearly. In this way, we avoid building subtle barriers that keep us separate. As we

learn to love and understand people more, we gain clear insights for how to deal productively with each situation that arises. It's easier for people to change and embrace new ideas when they feel our love and support.

This isn't always easy! I remember how I had to put this principle to the test during an extended publicity tour in Great Britain for *Sharing Nature with Children*. I arrived at a London radio station for a Sunday morning interview, and the disk jockey was playing Heavy Metal rock music. Ten people were sitting around waiting to be interviewed, but the DJ seemed interested only in interviewing himself. He talked in a self-important manner and moved quickly from one guest to the next, using the interviews to show off his cleverness.

My first reaction was disappointment that I'd wasted a wonderful Sunday morning to come here, when I'd given up an invitation to go birding and see many new species. I felt myself mentally rejecting the situation. Fighting down my initial response, I decided I might as well try and make the best of the situation, since I was already there.

As my interview began, I could see that the DJ wasn't interested in my book or me, and that the interview was going to be over in record time. But knowing that the English have a great fondness for nature, and that my interviewer obviously loved to talk, I asked him if he'd had any memorable childhood nature experiences. Suddenly his face lit up, his voice and manner changed, and he talked on and on enthusiastically about growing up in the countryside. He talked for about eight minutes, then, remembering that other guests were waiting, he concluded by saying, "We often forget how important nature is to us in our busy, hectic lives. *Sharing Nature with Children* is a marvelous book. I recommend it highly if you want to bring nature back into your life." I was amazed by his hearty endorsement —he had never even opened the book!

The single most vital key for bringing out the best in people is the inspiration we ourselves are feeling. An outdoor educator once told me that he used to think that the success of a hike depended on how sensitive and well-prepared the children were, but that he'd begun to notice that whenever *he* felt inspired and full of wonder, the class— even a difficult class—always had a wonderful time. He said he'd noticed also that whenever he wasn't feeling enthusiastic, no matter how good the group was, the hike wasn't particularly special. He said he'd begun to see that the teacher's inspiration was the *central* factor in creating meaningful nature experiences for others.

To communicate wonder, we must have a spirit of wonder. A leader who's filled with wonder, joy, and love for the natural world draws these good feelings out of others. They want eagerly to experience them for themselves.

Albert Schweitzer was once asked by his new medical students what was the best way to teach. He replied, "There are three ways of teaching: Number one—example. Number two—example. And number three—example." One individual, whose heart is filled with love and reverence for nature, can make ecological attitudes come alive for others as nothing else can. The important role of our personal example shouldn't be viewed in a self-conscious way, but should be taken simply as a personal responsibility to help ourselves and others grow more fully aware of our oneness with all life.

Before leading an outdoor class, it's a good idea to spend at least a few minutes by yourself communing with nature so that your teaching will be imbued with genuine enthusiasm and love. You'll find, too, that when you take a few moments to feel calm, joyful, and loving toward nature, you'll treat people in the same way. When we relate to the highest in people, we create an atmosphere that helps them too feel the highest.

———————◆———————

This aspect of nature education is so important that I devoted a whole book to the subject of personal inspiration. The book, Listening to Nature, *contains short quotations from great naturalists, along with stories and activities aimed at helping the reader turn inspiring ideas into personal experience. If you are interested in working consciously to deepen your relationship with nature,* Listening to Nature *should be of great benefit.*

APPENDIX A

THE MAN WHO PLANTED HOPE *and* GREW HAPPINESS

by *Jean Giono*

OR A HUMAN CHARACTER to reveal truly exceptional qualities, one must have the good fortune to be able to observe its performance over many years. If this performance is devoid of all egoism, if its guiding motive is unparalleled generosity, if it is absolutely certain that there is no thought of recompense and that, in addition, it has left its visible mark upon the earth, then there can be no mistake.

About forty years ago I was taking a long trip on foot over mountain heights quite unknown to tourists in that ancient region where the Alps thrust down into Provence. All this, at the time I embarked upon my long walk through these deserted regions, was barren and colorless land. Nothing grew there but wild lavender.

I was crossing the area at its widest point, and after three days' walking found myself in the midst of unparalleled desolation. I camped near the vestiges of an abandoned village. I had run out of water the day before, and had to find some. These clustered houses, although in ruins, like an old wasps' nest, suggested that there must once have been a spring or well here. There was, indeed, a spring, but it was dry. The five or six houses, roofless, gnawed by wind and rain, the tiny chapel with its crumbling steeple, stood about like the houses and chapels in living villages, but all life had vanished.

It was a fine June day, brilliant with sunlight, but over this unsheltered land, high in the sky, the wind blew with unendurable ferocity. It growled over the carcasses of the houses like a lion disturbed at its meal. I had to move my camp.

After five hours' walking I had still not found water, and there was nothing to give me any hope of finding any. All about me was the same dryness, the same coarse grasses. I thought I glimpsed in the distance a small black silhouette, upright, and took it for the trunk of a solitary tree. In any case I started towards it. It was a shepherd. Thirty sheep were lying about him on the baking earth.

He gave me a drink from his watergourd and, a little later, took me to his cottage in a fold of the plain. He drew his water—excellent water—from a very deep natural well above which he had constructed a primitive winch.

The man spoke little. This is the way of those who live alone, but one felt that he was sure of himself, and confident in his assurance. That was unexpected in this barren country. He lived, not in a cabin, but in a real house built of stone that bore plain evidence of how his own efforts had reclaimed the ruin he had found there on his arrival. His roof was strong and sound. The wind on its tiles made the sound of the sea upon its shores.

The place was in order, the dishes washed, the floor swept, his rifle oiled; his soup was boiling over the fire. I noticed then that he was cleanly shaved, that all his buttons were firmly sewed on, that his clothing had been mended with the meticulous care that makes the mending invisible. He shared his soup with me and afterwards, when I offered my tobacco pouch, he told me that he did not smoke. His dog, as silent as himself, was friendly without being servile.

It was understood from the first that I should spend the night there; the nearest village was still more than a day and a half away. And besides I was perfectly familiar with the nature of the rare villages in that region. There were four or five of them scattered well apart from each other on these mountain slopes, among white oak thickets, at the extreme end of the wagon roads. They were inhabited by charcoal-burners, and the living was bad. Families, crowded together in a climate that is excessively harsh both in winter and in summer, found no escape from the unceasing conflict of personalities. Irrational ambition reached inordinate proportions in the continual desire for escape. The men took their wagonloads of charcoal to the town, then returned.

The soundest characters broke under the perpetual grind. The women nursed their grievances. There was rivalry in everything, over the price of charcoal as over a pew in the church. And over all there was the wind, also ceaseless to rasp upon the nerves. There were epidemics of suicide and frequent cases of insanity, usually homicidal.

The shepherd went to fetch a small sack and poured out a heap of acorns on the table. He began to inspect them, one by one, with great concentration, separating the good from the bad. I smoked my pipe. I did offer to help him. He told me that it was his job. And in fact, seeing the care he devoted to the task, I did not insist. That was the whole of our conversation. When he had set aside a large enough pile of good acorns he counted them out by tens, meanwhile eliminating the small ones or those which were slightly cracked, for now he examined them more closely. When he had thus selected one hundred perfect acorns he stopped and he went to bed.

There was peace in being with this man. The next day I asked if I might rest here for a day. He found it quite natural—or, to be more exact, he gave me the impression that nothing could startle him. The rest was not absolutely necessary, but I was interested and wished to know more about him. He opened the pen and led his flocks to pasture. Before leaving, he plunged his sack of carefully selected and counted acorns into a pail of water. I noticed that he carried for a stick an iron rod as thick as my thumb and about a yard and a half long. Resting myself by walking, I followed a path parallel to his. His pasture was in a valley. He left the little flock in the charge of the dog and climbed towards where I stood. I was afraid that he was about to rebuke me for my indiscretion, but it was not that at all: this was the way he was going, and he invited me to go along if I had nothing better to do. He climbed to the top of the ridge about a hundred yards away.

There he began thrusting his iron rod into the earth, making a hole in which he planted an acorn; then he refilled the hole. He was planting oak trees. I asked him if the land belonged to him. He answered no. Did he know whose it was? He did not. He supposed it was community property, or perhaps belonged to people who cared nothing about it. He was not interested in finding out whose it was. He planted his hundred acorns with the greatest care. After the midday meal he resumed his planting. I suppose I must have been fairly insistent in my questioning, for he answered me. For three years he had been planting trees in this wilderness. He had planted 100,000. Of these, 20,000 had sprouted. Of the

20,000 he still expected to lose about half to rodents or to the unpredictable designs of Providence. There remained 10,000 oak trees to grow where nothing had grown before.

That was when I began to wonder about the age of this man. He was obviously over fifty. Fifty-five, he told me. His name was Elzéard Bouffier. He had once had a farm in the lowlands. There he had had his life. He had lost his only son, then his wife. He had withdrawn into this solitude, where his pleasure was to live leisurely with his lambs and his dog. It was his opinion that this land was dying for want of trees. He added that, having no very pressing business of his own, he had resolved to remedy this state of affairs.

Since I was at that time, in spite of my youth, leading a solitary life, I understood how to deal gently with solitary spirits. But my very youth forced me to consider the future in relation to myself and to a certain quest for happiness. I told him that in thirty years his 10,000 oaks would be magnificent. He answered quite simply that if God granted him life, in thirty years he would have planted so many more that these 10,000 would be like a drop of water in the ocean.

Besides, he was now studying the reproduction of beech trees and had a nursery of seedlings grown from beechnuts near his cottage. The seedlings, which he protected from his sheep with a wire fence, were very beautiful. He was also considering birches for the valleys where, he told me, there was a certain amount of moisture
a few yards below the surface
of the soil.

The next day
we parted.

HE FOLLOWING YEAR came the War of 1914, in which I was involved for the next five years. An infantryman hardly had time for reflecting upon trees. To tell the truth, the thing itself had made no impression upon me; I had considered it as a hobby, a stamp collection, and forgotten it.

The war over, I found myself possessed of a tiny demobilization bonus and a huge desire to breathe fresh air for a while. It was with no other objective that I again took the road to the barren lands.

The countryside had not changed. However, beyond the deserted village I glimpsed in the distance a sort of greyish mist that covered the mountaintops like a carpet. Since the day before, I had begun to think again of the shepherd tree-planter. "Ten thousand oaks," I reflected, "really take up quite a bit of space." I had seen too many men die during those five years not to imagine easily that Elzéard Bouffier was dead, especially since, at twenty, one regards men of fifty as old men with nothing left to do but die. He was not dead. As a matter of fact he was extremely spry. He had changed jobs. Now he had only four sheep but, instead, a hundred beehives. He had got rid of the sheep because they threatened his young trees. For, he told me (and I saw for myself), the war had disturbed him not at all. He had imperturbably continued to plant.

The oaks of 1910 were then ten years old and taller than either of us. It was an impressive spectacle. I was literally speechless and, as he did not talk, we spent the whole day walking in silence through his forest. In three sections, it measured eleven kilometers in length and three kilometers at its greatest width. When you remembered that all this had sprung from the hands and the soul of this one man, without technical resources, you understood that men could be as effectual as God in realms other than that of destruction.

He had pursued his plan, and beech trees as high as my shoulder, spreading out as far as the eye could reach, confirmed it. He showed me handsome clumps of birch planted

five years before—that is, in 1915, when I had been fighting at Verdun. He had set them out in all the valleys where he had guessed—and rightly—that there was moisture almost at the surface of the ground. They were as delicate as young girls, and very well established.

Creation seemed to come about in a sort of chain reaction. He did not worry about it; he was determinedly pursuing his task in all its simplicity; but as we went back towards the village I saw water flowing in brooks that had been dry since the memory of man. This was the most impressive result of chain reaction that I had seen. These dry streams had once, long ago, run with water. Some of the dreary villages I mentioned before had been built on the sites of ancient Roman settlements, traces of which still remained; and archaeologists, exploring there, had found fishhooks where, in the twentieth century, cisterns were needed to assure a small supply of water.

The wind, too, scattered seeds. As the water reappeared, so there reappeared willows, rushes, meadows, gardens, flowers, and a certain purpose in being alive. But the transformation took place so gradually that it became part of the pattern without causing any astonishment. Hunters, climbing into the wilderness in pursuit of hares or wild boar, had of course noticed the sudden growth of little trees, but had attributed it to some caprice of the earth. That is why no one meddled with Elzéard Bouffier's work. If he had been detected he would have had opposition. He was undetectable. Who in the villages or in the administration could have dreamed of such perseverance in a magnificent generosity?

To have anything like a precise idea of this exceptional character one must not forget that he worked in total solitude: so total that, towards the end of his life, he lost the habit of speech. Or perhaps it was that he saw no need for it.

In 1933 he received a visit from a forest ranger who notified him of an order against lighting fires out of doors for fear of endangering the growth of this *natural* forest. It was the first time, the man told him naively, that he had ever heard of a forest growing of its own accord. At that time Bouffier was about to plant beeches at a spot some twelve kilometers from

his cottage. In order to avoid travelling back and forth—for he was then seventy-five—he planned to build a stone cabin right at the plantation. The next year he did so.

In 1935 a whole delegation came from the Government to examine the "natural forest." There was a high official from the Forest Service, a Deputy, technicians. There was a great deal of ineffectual talk. It was decided that something must be done and, fortunately, nothing was done except the only helpful thing: the whole forest was placed under the protection of the State, and charcoal burning prohibited. For it was impossible not to be captivated by the beauty of those young trees in the fullness of health, and they cast their spell over the Deputy himself.

A friend of mine was among the forestry officers of the delegation. To him I explained the mystery. One day the following week we went together to see Elzéard Bouffier. We found him hard at work, some ten kilometers from the spot where the inspection had taken place.

This forester was not my friend for nothing. He was aware of values. He knew how to keep silent. I delivered the eggs I had brought as a present. We shared our lunch among the three of us and spent several hours in wordless contemplation of the countryside.

In the direction from which we had come the slopes were covered with trees twenty to twenty-five feet tall. I remembered how the land had looked in 1913: a desert...Peaceful, regular toil, the vigorous mountain air, frugality and, above all, serenity in the spirit had endowed this old man with awe-inspiring health. He was one of God's athletes. I wondered how many more acres he was going to cover with trees.

Before leaving my friend simply made a brief suggestion about certain species of trees that the soil here seemed particularly suited for. He did not force the point. "For the very good reason," he told me later, "that Bouffier knows more about it than I do." At the end of an hour's walking—having turned it over in his mind—he added, "He knows a lot more about it than anybody. He's discovered a wonderful way to be happy!"

It was thanks to this officer that not only the forest but also

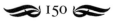

the happiness of the man was protected. He delegated three rangers to the task, and so terrorized them that they remained proof against all the bottles of wine the charcoal-burners could offer.

The only serious danger to the work occurred during the War of 1939. As cars were being run on gazogenes (wood-burning generators), there was never enough wood. Cutting was started among the oaks of 1910, but the area was so far from any railway that the enterprise turned out to be financially unsound. It was abandoned. The shepherd had seen nothing of it. He was thirty kilometers away, peacefully continuing his work, ignoring the war of 1939 as he had ignored that of 1914.

 SAW ELZÉARD BOUFFIER for the last time in June of 1945. He was then eighty-seven. I had started back along the route through the wastelands; but now, in spite of the disorder in which the war had left the country, there was a bus running between the Durance Valley and the mountain. I attributed the fact that I no longer recognized the scenes of my earlier journeys to this relatively speedy transportation. It took the name of a village to convince me that I was actually in that region that had been all ruins and desolation.

The bus put me down at Vergons. In 1913 this hamlet of ten or twelve houses had three inhabitants. They had been savage creatures, hating one another, living by trapping game, little removed, physically and morally, from the conditions of prehistoric man. All about them nettles were feeding upon the remains of abandoned houses. Their condition had been beyond hope. For them, nothing but to await death—a situation which rarely predisposes to virtue.

Everything was changed. Even the air. Instead of the harsh dry winds that used to attack me, a gentle breeze was blowing, laden with scents. A sound like water came from the mountains; it was the wind in the forest; most amazing of all, I heard the actual sound of water falling into a pool. I saw that a fountain had been built, that it flowed freely and—what touched me most—that someone had planted a linden beside it, a linden that must have been four years old, already in full leaf, the incontestable symbol of resurrection.

Besides, Vergons bore evidence of labor at the sort of undertaking for which hope is required. Hope, then, had returned. Ruins had been cleared away, dilapidated walls torn down and five houses restored. Now there were twenty-eight inhabitants, four of them young married couples. The new houses, freshly plastered, were surrounded by gardens where vegetables and flowers grew in orderly confusion, cabbages and roses, leeks and snapdragons, celery and anemones. It was now a village where one would like to live.

From that point I went on foot. The war just finished had not allowed the full blooming of life, but Lazarus was out of the tomb. On the lower slopes of the mountain I saw little fields of barley and rye; deep in that narrow valley the meadows were turning green.

It has taken only the eight years since then for the whole countryside to glow with health and prosperity. On the site of the ruins I had seen in 1913 now stand neat farms, cleanly plastered, testifying to a happy and comfortable life. The old streams, fed by the rains and snows that the forest conserves, are flowing again. Their waters have been channeled. On each farm, in groves of maples, fountain pools overflow on to carpets of fresh mint. Little by little the villages have been rebuilt. People from the plains, where land is costly, have settled here, bringing youth, motion, the spirit of adventure. Along the roads you meet hearty men and women, boys and girls who understand laughter and have recovered a taste for picnics. Counting the former population, unrecognizable now that they live in comfort, more than 10,000 people owe their happiness to Elzéard Bouffier.

When I reflect that one man, armed only with his own physical and moral resources, was able to cause this land of Canaan to spring from the wasteland, I am convinced that, in

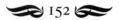

spite of everything, humanity is admirable. But when I com-
pute the unfailing greatness of spirit and the tenacity of
benevolence that it must have taken to achieve this result, I
am taken with an immense respect for that old and unlearned
peasant who was able to complete a work worthy of God.

Elzéard Bouffier died peacefully in 1947 at the hospice in
Banon.

—FRIENDS OF NATURE
BROOKSVILLE, MAINE, 1967

APPENDIX B

FLOW LEARNING ACTIVITY CHART

All of the activities in *Sharing Nature with Children, Sharing Nature with Children II,* and *Listening to Nature* are listed here, under the stages of Flow Learning for which they can be used most effectively. The chart should help you design your Flow Learning sessions. [Note: page references are to the second edition of *Sharing Nature with Children.*]

1. Awaken Enthusiasm

Sharing Nature with Children
Animal Clue Relay—92
Animal Game—72
Animal Parts—90
Bat & Moth—108
Catch the Horse—100
Identification Game—76
Noah's Ark—89
Noses—70
Owls & Crows—78
Predator-Prey—62
Pyramid of Life—54

Webbing—60
What Animal Am I?—75
Wild Animal Scramble—86
Wildman in the Alders—104

Sharing Nature with Children II
Animal Clue Game—52
Build a Tree—62
Getting Acquainted—72
Habitat—70
Natural Processes—60
Nature Bingo—66

2. Focus Attention

Sharing Nature with Children
Camouflage—102
Colors—41
Micro Hike—50
Plant Succession Crawl—64
Recon-Hike—122
Scavenger Hunt—84
Sleeping Miser—106
Sounds—40
Survival Hike—148

Tree Silhouettes—82
Unnature Trail—42
Watcher of the Road—110

Sharing Nature with Children II
Animals, Animals!—81
Barefoot Walk—78
Sound Map—74
Wilderness Trail—76

3. Direct Experience

4. Share Inspiration

APPENDIX C

RECOMMENDED READING

These books contain many inspirational stories and insights that you can share with others.

Boone, J. Allen. *Kinship with All Life*. New York: Harper & Row Publishers, 1954

Brown, Tom. *Tom Brown's Field Guide to Nature Observation & Tracking*. New York: Berkley Books, 1983

Brown, Tom. *The Tracker*. New York: Berkley Books, 1978

Byrd, Baylor and Peter Parnall. *Another Way to Listen*. New York: Charles Scribner's Sons, 1978

Carson, Rachel L. *The Sense of Wonder*. New York: Harper & Row Publishers, 1956

Clark, Glenn. *The Man Who Talks with the Flowers: The Life Story of George Washington Carver*. Saint Paul, Minnesota: Macalester Park Publishing Co., 1939

Elliot, Lawrence. *George Washington Carver*. Englewood Cliffs, New Jersey: Prentice-Hall, Inc., 1966 (Out of print)

Findhorn Community. *The Findhorn Garden*. New York: Harper & Row, Publishers, 1975

Fulop-Miller, Rene. *The Saints that Moved the World*: Saint Francis of Assisi, pages 153–271. Salem, New Hampshire: Ayers Co., Publishers, Inc., 1985

George, Jean. *My Side of the Mountain*. New York: E.P. Dutton & Co., 1959

Giono, Jean. *The Man Who Planted Hope and Grew Happiness*. Brooksville, Maine: Friends of Nature, 1967

Jones, Ron. *The Acorn People*. New York: Bantam Books, 1977

McLuhan, T. C. *Touch the Earth*. New York: Promontory Press, 1971

Muir, John. *Stickeen*. Berkeley: Heyday Books, 1981

Muir, John. *The Wilderness World of John Muir*. Boston: Houghton Mifflin Publishers, 1954

Stapleton, Laurence, editor. *H.D. Thoreau: A Writer's Journal*. New York: Dover Publications, 1960

Storm, Hyemeyohsts. *Seven Arrows*. New York: Ballantine Books, Inc., 1973

Wolfe, Linnie Marsh. *The Life of John Muir: Son of the Wilderness*. Madison, Wisconsin: The University of Wisconsin Press, 1945

RESOURCES FOR TEACHERS

Hidden Villa Environmental Education. *Manure to Meadow to Milkshake*. Hidden Villa, Inc., Drawer AH, Los Altos, CA, 1978

Knapp, Clifford E., and Goodman, Joel. *Humanizing Environmental Education*. Martinsville, Indiana: American Camping Association, 1981

Margolin, Malcolm. *The Earth Manual*. Berkeley: Heyday Books, 1975

Nature Scope. Washington, D.C.: National Wildlife Federation, 1986

Project Wild. Salina Star Route, Boulder, Colorado, 80302: Western Regional Environmental Education Council, 1986

Van Matre, Steve. *Acclimatizing*. Martinsville, Indiana: American Camping Association, 1974

Walters, J. Donald. *Education for Life*. Nevada City, California: Crystal Clarity, Publishers, 1986

Animal Town Game Co. Catalog (cooperative and noncompetitive board games, and outdoor and educational playthings and books). P.O. Box 2002, Santa Barbara, CA 93120

REFERENCES FOR ACTIVITIES:

ANIMAL CLUE GAME:—Frogs:
Time Life Television Book. *Reptiles & Amphibians*. Time Life Films, 1976
Hummingbirds:
Skutch, Alexander F. *The Life of the Hummingbird*. New York: Crown Publishers, Inc., 1973
Spiders:
Walther, Tom. *A Spider Might*. San Francisco/ New York: Sierra

Club Books/Charles Scribner's Sons, 1978

Levi, Herbert W. and Lorna R., and Zim, Herbert S. *Spiders and Their Kin*. New York: Golden Press, 1968

Whales:

Valencic, Joe and Robin. *Whale Watchers Guide*. Box 823, Dana Point, California: Joe Valencic, c/o Quest Marine Research

GETTING ACQUAINTED:

Knapp, Clifford E., and Goodman, Joel. *Humanizing Environmental Education*. Martinsville, Indiana: American Camping Association, 1981

SOUND MAP:

Tribe, David. Gould League, New South Wales, Australia

MYSTERY ANIMAL:

Ayensu, Edward S. *Jungles*. New York: Crown Publishers, Inc., 1980

Weyer Jr., Edward M. *Strangest Creatures on Earth*. New York: Sheridan House, 1953

International Wildlife. Washington, D. C.: National Wildlife Federation, Jan./Feb. 1986, Volume 16, Number 1

International Wildlife. Washington, D. C.: National Wildlife Federation, May/June 1983, Volume 13, Number 3

TREE IMAGERY & BUILD A TREE:

Platt, Rutherford. *The Great American Forest*. Englewood Cliffs, New Jersey: Prentice-Hall, Inc., 1965

NATURE MEDITATIONS:

Cornell, Joseph. *Listening to Nature*. 14618 Tyler Foote Road, Nevada City, CA 95959: Dawn Publications, 1987

APPENDIX D

INDEX TO QUOTATIONS
Alphabetical by Author

Skutch—from *The Life of Hummingbirds* by Alexander Skutch. Crown Publishers, 1973

Thoreau—Henry David Thoreau

Weyer—from *Strangest Creatures on Earth* by Edward M. Weyer, Jr. Sheridan House, Inc., 1953

White—from *The Once and Future King* by T.H. White. Putnam Company, 1966

Winnebago Indians

CREDITS:

BOOK DESIGN AND PRODUCTION:
Josh Gitomer

ILLUSTRATORS:
Elizabeth Ann Kelley—5, 51, 59, 66, 69, 80, 108, 116, 159
Judy Daniel—142, 146/147, 153
Illustrator unknown—52/53

PHOTOGRAPHERS:
Ollie Atkins—33
George Beinhorn—title page, 20, 21, 22, 23, 24, 25, 26, 28, 30, 41, 46, 53, 75, 86, 92, 102/103, 104, 118/119, 124/125, 128/129
Robert Belous—78
E. Haanel Cassidy—16/17, 38
Joseph Cornell—6/7, 91, 96/97, 162
Louis Feinman—½ title page
Robert Frutos—165
Paul Green—163
Wayne Green—Back cover, 111
John Hendrickson—Front cover, 10, 72, 133
Dan Hoover—138
Cliff McDivitt—62, 115
National Park Service—12
Rodney Polden—60, 77, 132/133
Lisa Yount—48/49, 65, 83 (all 3), 163
Photographer unknown—56, 71, 86

ACKNOWLEDGEMENTS:

I AM GRATEFUL, first and foremost, to my wife, for her keen sense of what is true, and how to communicate it accurately and enjoyably to others. The clear expression of many of the book's ideas is due in a large part to her efforts.

I would also like to thank George Beinhorn for his long-term enthusiasm for my work and his editorial expertise. His efforts have been truly a labor of love.

Living in an intentional community like Ananda World Brotherhood Village has many advantages. One is the wonderful sense of support one feels in one's life and work. This book, like my others, shows how the sum of several people's efforts can be much richer than if a single person had worked on the project alone. I would like to thank these members of the community for their suggestions and support: Jim Van Cleave, Sheila Rush, Jay Casbon, Helen Purcell, Alan Heubert, Peter and Karen MacDow, Clara Evans, Vaughn-Paul Manley, Bruce Malnor, Hayward Crewe, Phyllis Novak, Happy Winingham, Paul Kelly and Asha Praver. Special thanks to J. Donald Walters, the founder of the Ananda community, for his inspiration and wisdom.

Thanks are due also to professors Rocky Rohwedder and Peter Corcoran for their many valuable comments.

Last, I would like to thank all those who have so enthusiastically participated in my workshops. This book couldn't have been written without you.

Sharing Nature Foundation

JOSEPH CORNELL and other teachers personally trained by him offer nature awareness workshops throughout the year through the Sharing Nature Foundation. These programs are based on Mr. Cornell's years of experience teaching nature awareness. They draw extensively on the activities and philosophy presented in the four-volume Sharing Nature Series: *Sharing Nature with Children, Sharing Nature with Children II, Journey to the Heart of Nature,* and *Listening to Nature.*

Every summer Joseph Cornell also conducts a week-long conference retreat in Northern California. Participants experience many ways of deepening their enjoyment of the natural world and come away with effective and inspirational tools they can use both professionally and personally.

In addition, Sharing Nature Worldwide is an international association of organizations and individuals using Cornell's philosophy and activities.

To find out more about Sharing Nature coordinators and programs in other countries, foreign translations of Cornell's books, and his schedule and workshops, please visit the Sharing Nature web site at http://www.sharingnature.com. To sponsor a program or workshop, or to find out more about the summer conference, write, e-mail, or call the Sharing Nature Foundation at 14618 Tyler Foote Road, Nevada City, CA 95959; sharingnature@telis.org; or telephone or fax: (530) 478-7650.

About the Author

FROM HIS EARLIEST YEARS, JOSEPH CORNELL has felt a sensitive attunement with the mysteries and beauties of nature. As a boy, he spent much time exploring the marshes, orchards, and mountains near his home in northern California.

Cornell has spent most of his adult life outdoors, too, showing others the wonders of nature. Joseph designed his own Bachelor of Science degree program in nature awareness at California State University in Chico. He received formal training as a naturalist with the National Audubon Society. Then, for seven years, he taught in public school outdoor education programs, and as a naturalist for the Boy Scouts of America. In 1979, he established the Sharing Nature Foundation to share his methods and philosophy with adults and teachers.

Today, as one of the world's leading nature educators, Cornell's workshops on nature awareness have been attended by tens of thousands of people around the globe. *Sharing Nature with Children,* the first in the Sharing Nature Series, has sold over 350,000 copies and has been translated into more than fifteen languages.

Discover the Seasons, by Diane Iverson, introduces the young child to the wonders of changing seasons in verse, plus seasonally appropriate activities and recipes.

With Love, to Earth's Endangered Peoples, by Virginia Kroll. All over the world, groups of people, like species of animals, are endangered. This book portrays several such peoples, with love. (Teacher's Guide available.)

Lifetimes, by David Rice, introduces some of nature's longest, shortest, and most unusual lifetimes, and what they have to teach us. This book teaches, but it also goes right to the heart. (Teacher's Guide available.)

A Drop Around the World, by Barbara Shaw McKinney, follows a single drop of water on its worldwide water cycle journey, inspiring respect for water's unique role on Earth. (Teacher's Guide available.)

A Swim through the Sea, by Kristin Joy Pratt. This young author-illustrator's alphabet format book uses delightful alliterative verse to introduce the ocean habitat. Similar habitat-based books by this author: *A Walk in the Rainforest* and *A Fly in the Sky.* (Teacher's Guides available.)

Teachers: ask about our *Sharing Nature with Children Series* **of teacher's guides,** by Bruce and Carol Malnor—a practical and creative way to incorporate Dawn's books into the school curriculum. Ask also for information about school visits by our authors and illustrators.

DAWN PUBLICATIONS is dedicated to inspiring in children a deeper understanding and appreciation for all life on Earth. For a copy of our catalog please call 800-545-7475. Please also visit our web site at www.dawnpub.com.

THE SHARING NATURE SERIES BY JOSEPH CORNELL

Sharing Nature with Children. The Classic Parents' and Teachers' Nature Awareness Guidebook.

Sharing Nature with Children II. The Sequel to the Classic Nature Awareness Guidebook (formerly *Sharing the Joy of Nature*).

Journey to the Heart of Nature. A Guided Exploration, especially for Young Adults. Through stories, activities and extended visits to a self-chosen special place in nature, Cornell conducts the reader to an ever-deepening appreciation of that place—and for all natural places.

John Muir: My Life with Nature. This unique "autobiography" of John Muir is told in many of his own words, compiled by Joseph Cornell, brimming with Muir's spirit and adventures. This book gives young adults an experience of a true hero.

With Beauty Before Me. This pocket-sized book for young adults and adults is filled with inspirational quotes, black and white photographs, and meditative-type activities that encourgae a sense of communion, serenity and loving interaction with the world of nature.

Listening to Nature. A Journey of Beauty into the Essence of Nature. A now-classic book for meditative and dynamic ways of achieving peace through nature—yet light, with stunning photographs and full of Cornell's irrepressible enthusiasm.

Sharing Nature with Children Video. Filmed in the High Sierras, Cornell shares his nature awareness teaching techniques as well as his exuberance in this beautiful 40-minute video.

The Sharing Nature Walk Audio Cassette. The audio companion to *Sharing Nature with Children*, contains teaching resources that can be used in the classroom, the home and the field to expand a child's awareness of nature.